Communication

Golden Nugget Methods to Communicate Effectively

Interpersonal, Influence, Social Skills and Listening

Ross Elkins

Ross Elkins

Ross Elkins

Please note the information contained within this document is for educational and entertainment purposes only. Every attempt has been made to provide accurate, up to date and reliable complete information. No warranties of any kind are expressed or implied. Readers acknowledge that the author is not engaging in the rendering of legal, financial, medical or professional advice.

By reading this document, the reader agrees that under no circumstances are we responsible for any losses, direct or indirect, which are incurred as a result of the use of information contained within this document, including, but not limited to, — errors, omissions, or inaccuracies.

Table of Contents

Introduction

It has been said many times that communication is one of the most important assets to living because it puts people together. The ability to transcend the barriers of this world and to actually impart your thoughts, knowledge, dreams, and desires to others around you forms the heart of communication. There's something truly magical about getting to know someone and letting him or her get to know you - to express yourself freely to another individual. It's an exhilarating experience and, most of all - it's absolutely necessary for the world we live in.

Yet, there's a fox in the henhouse. While communication is so vital and now, more than ever, communication with others is so simple and easy that children are proficient at it, we've lost something. We are experiencing generations all around us who know nothing other than the world of social networking and cell phones, worlds that don't require that personal touch in communication. Whether you're just a person stuck in their private cocoon, or a person who wants to make a connection outside of their phone or their computer, this book is for you.

What I want to enthuse you with is the sense of wonder and excitement that communicating with others can give you. The ability to meet new friends, strike up conversations and share with others what's really on your mind is what I'm going to share with you inside these pages. By the time you're done with this book, I want you to know exactly what you're going to do to start sharing with the world who you are and why they should get know you.

But, this isn't limited to the shy and the socially isolated. Maybe you're just looking for a boost in your ability to make a connection with others. You might already be sociable, but you really want to stand out and get people's attention. When you speak, you want all eyes falling on you. Well, there's a way you can get that and I'm going to share that with you.

Of course, there are always those moments in life where we're going to have to stand up in front of a bunch of people and whether you know them or not is going to be irrelevant. All that matters is what you're about to say. Well, I'm going to give you tips on spreading influence and getting your words to come out right when you're talking to large groups of people.

Enough of this! We're wasting valuable time! There's a whole world out there waiting for you to go introduce yourself to it. So let's not waste another second.

Communication

Ross Elkins

Chapter 1
What is Communication

Communication is an informed inclination. In any case, while the greater part are imagined with the physical ability to talk, not all can pass on well unless they make remarkable attempts to make and refine this capacity further. Constantly, we carry the straightforwardness with which we talk with each other for in truth, to such a degree, to the point that we now and again disregard how complex the procedure of correspondence really is.

Communication is essentially the process of effectively transferring or conveying a message or messages to another person. Take note that it's not just making sure the other person receives the message but also he or she understands it clearly. It's easy to let the other person simply receive the message – you can write an email, text, call or personally talk to him or her. Making sure your message is understood can be a challenge.

An example of this is my friend Perry. He and I go along way back so it's safe to assume that we know each other very well. So well that often times when we're caught in unexpected situations, we just gesture to each other with a nod or a raised eyebrow and the other person would immediately get what the other is trying to say. But that isn't to say our communication is perfect. There'd be times where I'd go "What were you thinking, man? You were supposed to say no when I raised my brows!" The way I sent the message was very easy – he certainly received the message. He just didn't "get" it.

Powerful Communication

The accomplishment of a person in a group depends extraordinarily on the degree to which he can participate in powerful correspondence. Defective correspondence in associations can prompt brought down proficiency and viability at the hierarchical and also individual level. Likewise the vast majority of the interpersonal grating can be followed to workforce correspondence. I remember one time when as part of my function in one of the biggest banks' risk management department, I had to call the attention of the head of the Treasury Group on account of his traders' breaching of a certain trading limit. So I promptly sent an email to him and the trader concerned. Protocol also dictates that I copy furnish the bank's President.

Next thing I knew, hell was breaking loose. My division manager and the Chief Risk Officer or CRO called an emergency meeting and asked me why I immediately emailed the Treasurer and the President about the breach. I should've informed him first before I did. Although I defended my self by saying the division's Board-approved policies and guidelines calls for the action I just did. The reply to my defense was "Here in our group, the practice is before informing the group concerned as well as the President of any breaches in trading limits, the CRO needs to be informed first." The inability to communicate effectively to me the "culture" when I first joined the group resulted in my taking the "wrong" action and has compromised our group's ability to do its job correctly or within acceptable protocols that day.

Communication, gotten from the Latin word "Communicare" which means to offer; is the procedure of transmitting data and comprehension. It is the transference of significance in the middle of people and the method for coming to, understanding and impacting others. Ability to impart relies upon the limit of a person to pass on thoughts also, sentiments to another to advance a sought reaction. Take note of the words "impart", "limit" and "reaction" and their importance in effective communications. Impart implies more than just letting the other person read, hear or see the message – it implies a transfer of your understanding of the message. As with the example of my friend Perry, he received my message when he saw my raised eyebrows but I wasn't able to impart to him what I meant by that message. Limit implies the communicators' capacity to relay the message in a way that the other person can easily understand. In the case again of me and Perry, that limit was the inability to speak the message directly to him because that person we were talking to can't find us out. That limit offered me non-verbal options or ability to transmit my message to Perry, which in that case were raised eyebrows. Lastly, reaction refers to the response we want from the other person. To the extent we are able to effectively impart our message given our limitations at the moment is the extent to which we can expect the other person to respond in the way we want or expect them to.

In administration, correspondence is a blend of individual characteristics and hierarchical angles. Effective interpersonal and inter-departmental communications need to take into consideration individuals' communication skills and the organization's communications protocols because any mismatches can create a logjam or constriction in the communications process. As with the case of my risk management experience that I shared with you earlier, the result of a mismatch between my personal communication skills and the group's unspoken protocols spelled disaster for that particular situation.

Great correspondence is vital for all associations as administration capacities in associations are completed through correspondence. When organizational correspondence is not efficient or logical, it can lead to serious productivity issues. Worse, it can even constitute a significant risk in terms of costly mistakes. Consider the case of Walden, a sales agent for a high-end office equipment manufacturing company.

Walden was on vacation when he accidentally met the President of a relatively large but starting up company. They hit it off very well and Walden found out that the starting up company urgently needs to acquire a hundreds of pieces of the equipment Walden's company is making. The President said he's already looking to sign a contract with a supplier the next morning though nothing's final yet. He asked Walden if he can quote a better offer and if he can give such a quote by end of the day, the transaction was his and the company's.

With much excitement, Walden calls the office. Oh no...it's a Sunday! No one is at work. He calls his boss but was informed that for transactions of that magnitude, they needed the company President's go ahead to give a formal quote. Since it's a Sunday and Walden's boss doesn't have the President's or the President's secretary's personal numbers, Walden didn't get approval and failed to land the deal. Because of his company's lack of a communications protocol for such situations, they missed out on the opportunity to land a deal that could've put the company back in the black after years of operating losses.

Compelling administration is an element of viable correspondence. If an organization's administrative functions are weak and inefficient, there would either be a very inefficient correspondence system or worse, none at all! Like the case of Walden earlier, his company's administration wasn't compelling enough to facilitate such a once-in-a-lifetime opportunity, which completely slipped from its hands. That's how important strong leadership and administration is when it comes to effectively communicating or corresponding.

Interpersonal communications is pretty much the same. You need to be able to administer the process of correspondence very well – in a compelling way – in order to elicit your desired response from the other person, which is what effective communications is about.

In addition disappointments in correspondence can be exorbitant for the association by method for decreased co-operation and ensuing sick feeling between representatives. Correspondence, to be successful, can't be a random procedure. It must be arranged and executed with the goal that it brings out the craved reaction. Correspondence in associations has the accompanying part:

- Helps in encouraging inspiration

- Aids in the capacity of control

- Provides data for deciding

- Gives vent to one's emotions

- Helps in the fulfillment of social needs

Process Of Communication

The procedure of correspondence between two people can be delineated beneath:

Input

Sender Message Receiver

Encoding Channel

The sender who conceptualizes the thought that is to be transmitted starts correspondence. This thought is encoded with the assistance of dialect, images and so on into a message. The sender is responsible for figuring out what particular language to use (English, Chinese, German or another local dialect), what image to conjure using the selected language (visual or literal) and how to incorporate other things that can make the message or correspondence more compelling, i.e., culturally relevant examples, figures of speech and the like.

The message, which is the result of encoding, is transmitted from the sender to the collector through a channel. Channel or medium can be physical vicinity (up close and personal talk) intuitive stations (phone, electronic media) individual static channel (updates, letters) or unoriginal static channels (general reports, brochures and so forth.). The choice of channels by which to transmit the message or correspondence is dependent on the recipient's personal background (age, race, culture from which he or she came from), social status, position and life experience. An example of this would be the end users of the reports I wrote when I was still employed – the company's Board of Directors. Knowing that these people are highly educated, very formal and are the top of our company's hierarchy, the medium by which I communicate to the them or correspond with them is through formal, written reports that go through several layers of management. As much as I'd just like to email them bullet points of the highlights of my reports, I can't. They need a formal write up that follows a certain template and flow as well as supporting schedules for such. Part of the medium also is presenting the report in person during meetings of the Board of Directors. Their positions, backgrounds and responsibilities dictate that there be no other way for them to better understand the importance and significance of the main points of my reports.

But if I present my initial findings or results of my work to my immediate boss, I don't need to create a formal report and PowerPoint slides. I can just email him bullet points of the highlights of my report and their supporting schedules and that's it. He only asks to meet with me if there are some points he can't understand even with in depth email explanation. Because of his status and position in the company as well as his responsibilities, a formal report isn't the optimal way for him to understand the fine details and important points of my report.

The best channel for communicating a message is still, and will always be, face to face. As needs be, eye to eye talk is viewed as wealthiest and indifferent static channel is thought to be the leanest. Why is this so?

Consider long-distance runners such as marathon runners and ultra-marathoners. Have you ever noticed that none of them are fat? Further, all of them are relatively lean, i.e., minimal body fat. Apart from fast metabolisms due to continuous running, they need to make sure they don't put on any extra body fat because it will slow them down and make them tire easier. Body fat presents impediments to optimal, i.e., fast, running.

It's the same with communications. The less impediments or middlemen there are, the better. Going directly to the person face-to-face, eye-to-eye couldn't be anymore direct. There is absolutely no risk of the medium failing to deliver the message and by delivering the message personally, you are in the position to immediately adjust your method of delivery because you can already see in that person's eyes and facial expression if he or she is getting it. Face-to-face communications also gives the receiver the benefit of immediately clarifying something that's not clear and so significantly improving his or her ability to understand your message and react or respond accordingly.

However for making correspondence proficient, the sender needs to pick the channel contingent on the direness and multifaceted nature of the thought that is imparted. In other words, the choice of channel should be dependent on or factor the importance, urgency and the content of the message to be transmitted. If your message contains offensive information, face-to-face channels may not be optimal as it may escalate into a fight and as such, it may be better to send a carefully thought and meticulously written one instead.

When the message is transmitted through the channel to the collector, he interprets it back to the thought and absorbs it. The adequacy of correspondence relies on the degree to which the sender has succeeded in making the recipient comprehend his thought. This can be assessed through input, where the recipient reacts to the sender as elucidations and questions. Input, which makes correspondence two-way, is critical since it serves to assess the adequacy of the correspondence.

Elements of Communication

Verbal correspondence

Verbal correspondence (vocal included) adds up to about 45% of our correspondence. It includes the utilization of dialect and significance (either oral or composed). Dialect or language is the more important part of verbal correspondence because it's the primary way people understand messages. Think of it this way: if I don't understand any Chinese dialects, you cannot structure your message or supplement it well enough for me to get what you're really trying to say if you persist in corresponding with me I n a Chinese dialect. Personally, I find a composed verbal correspondence a much better significance because I'm the type of person who communicates thoughts and ideas best when given enough time to craft a message. Oral correspondences are quite difficult for a person such as me who isn't as quick on his feet as other people are. For other people, though, oral works better as it gives both parties the benefit of real time clarification and correction, should there be any miscommunication or mistakes in the correspondence. Of course, there are trade-offs to both. For oral significance, you don't have the benefit of being able to thoroughly think about the message you're going to communicate if it's spontaneous or extemporaneous. If you're reading your written message orally to the person or people concerned, it's impact may be a bit diminished at sounds less sincere than extemporaneous. On the other hand, the trade-off for composed verbal correspondences is it's a bit more tedious to clarify or correct parts of the message that may be unclear or mistaken. Because the parties aren't face to face, it will take time for the other party to respond to any clarifications or objections that the recipient may have to the original message. It may also run the risk miscommunication, especially if the recipient thinks he or she got the message right because the sender isn't there to personally see the gestures or facial reactions.

Typically the words utilized as a part of correspondence are concrete or theoretical. Concrete words speak about an item (e.g. Seat) and subsequently pass on thoughts effortlessly. This is because concrete words are those that can actually be experienced or may have already been experienced by the other person's senses, i.e., sight, touch, hearing, taste and smell. It's easier to understand messages with concrete words because there's something you can immediately compare it to for reference.

Theoretical or unique words on the other hand, have a fabricated unambiguity since the thoughts passed on by such words are subjective, i.e., mean different things to different people unlike a seat. As such, the adequacy of correspondence is being referred to (e.g. magnificence, knowledge and so forth.). Therefore, while concrete words can be contrasted with a sharp apparatus, theoretical words are regularly contrasted with an obtuse instrument.

Part of languages is additionally critical in deciding the viability of correspondence. While languages help to convey effortlessly in a homogeneous gathering, unnecessary utilization of them can impede correspondence. Utilization of languages must be minimized while imparting to somebody who is not acquainted with the terms. What does this mean?

I remember two specific instances when I took the same subject, one in college and the other during my post-graduate studies. The subject in question was statistics. As a college freshman, I was hardly familiar with how businesses work, particularly the product manufacturing processes. So when the lessons in statistics were being taught using examples, I couldn't get it. The teacher was instructing the class in English, a language that I'm very, very familiar with. But because the examples given utilized words that I found to be too technical as a student, I struggled and barely passed the course.

Fast forward years later. I've already worked several years in the financial services industry and was taking my master's degree in finance. Once again, I had to take up statistics. Since I barely passed the course as an undergraduate many years before, it's safe to say that I took the subject again as if I knew nothing about it – like I was a beginner. But guess what? I aced the subject and was even among the top of the class. What happened?

Two things. First, several years' worth of experience in the business sector familiarized me with the concepts I weren't familiar with back as an undergrad. When the professor explained statistical concepts through examples, I was now able to relate to those examples and as such, started to understand the concepts easier and better. Second, the professor was a very wise and practical man. Compared to my college professor, he limited the use of technical words only to instances where there was no layman's term equivalent. In doing so, he made the lessons more relatable and easier to grasp. That's how I aced the subject. The professor utilized a very viable way of corresponding or communicating the lesson with the class.

Verbal correspondence gets to be successful through the decision of right words & accentuation of the same. There ought to be an ideal utilization of stops, non-words and expressions on the grounds that extreme utilization of these prompts diversion of the beneficiary. This is what separates great oral communicators from mediocre or ineffective ones. Gestures, body language, tone of voice and facial expressions have a subtle but very powerful way of sending messages across or reinforcing what is being communicated verbally. In fact, what is verbally communicated can often times be nullified by non-verbal communications.

I love the glam metal bands of the late 80's and early 90's. The reason I love those bands is because how powerfully emotional their songs were. If the song was about angst, boy can you feel it. If they were singing a ballad, you'd feel the intense romantic emotions behind the vocals and music – as if you knew what they were talking about. In particular, one of my favorites was Skid Row.

Skid Row's vocalist, Sebastian Bach, was as gifted an artist as one can come. He's ruggedly handsome, has an insanely wide vocal range and knows when to accentuate the highlights of the songs by use of various vocal techniques such as growling, mellowing and screaming, among others. He employed those techniques to increase or decrease a song's emotional intensity at the right times. The band itself also utilizes stops, crescendos and speed – among other things – to accentuate certain emotional highlights of their songs. In other words, the band members were masters in utilizing expressions, stops and other verbal cues to bring their listeners to an emotional roller coaster ride with their songs and performances. They were very excellent communicators that allowed them to consistently receive their desired responses from their fans.

Non-verbal Communication

Non-verbal correspondence is the cognizant and oblivious body developments in correspondence that couple with physical and natural environment. Non-verbal correspondences are those that are not communicated orally, or in composing and incorporates human components connected with correspondence. These structure a vital and inescapable part of the aggregate correspondence process in light of the fact that it compliments and substitutes verbal correspondence.

In fact, non-verbal communications seem to comprise bulk of effective interpersonal communications. Interpersonal communications experts generally agree that verbal communications on average comprise just 10% to 20% of effective interpersonal communications and the remaining 80% to 90% is comprised of non-verbal correspondence. As such, a decent communicator ought to have the right stance, outward appearance and non-verbal communication that are tuned in to the words talked. Absence of co-appointment in the middle of verbal and nonverbal substance of correspondence would just befuddle the beneficiary. So while imparting, consideration ought to be taken to guarantee a fitting mix in the middle of words and activities.

In organizational, formal communications, non-verbals aren't as important. It's because such communications tend to concentrate on written forms such as memos, reports and emails.

Listening & Feedback

Listening, which embodies hearing, going to, understanding, and recalling can encourage the viability of correspondence. Listening can be pleasurable, discriminative or basic relying upon the level of use of brain. Audience needs to utilize the fitting sort of listening relying upon the circumstance and nature of the message.

Correspondences or communications are enhanced through good listening because when you pay enough attention and listen, you get very valuable insights as to how you can best communicate your message for optimal understanding by the other party. Sometimes, the other party says something that makes or breaks your ability to effectively communicate to him and her and if you weren't listening, you'll miss it completely.

I remember a time a friend of mine was asking me for advice as to where to invest his extra money. As he was telling me about his financial investing background and experience, a really cool bike passed us by and caught my attention. It was so timely that as I focused my attention for a second or two on the bike that passed by, my friend said he's not familiar with binary options as an investment. And having completely missed that detail, I kept on explaining the basics of binary options to him as if he had at least some basic knowledge of the thing. Guess what? He asked me to repeat the whole thing only this time, in more basic detail – in layman's terms. I spoke in the same language or dialect that he understood but because I bombarded him with technical details and too much information, he wasn't able to understand my message fully and didn't respond the way I expected him to, which is to invest in binary options.

And that, my friend, is why you should learn how to listen well if you want to effectively communicate to people.

Legitimate listening obliges a sensible foundation nature, right mentalities, interest, objectivity, tolerance and compatibility with the sender. Nonappearance of compatibility with the sender frequently prompts snare listening where the beneficiary listens just till he gets a point for contention after which his primary goal would be to intrude on the correspondence. Absence of enthusiasm for the subject talked by a man with whom we have compatibility would in some cases make us utilize pseudo tuning in. Proper audience reaction serves as an implication by which input is judged. The input ought to be convenient and useful.

We will discuss more on this on the Listening Chapter.

Ross Elkins

Chapter 2
The Personable Person

When you think about communication, what is it that you mean? How do some people manage to take a deep breath and just plunge into the waters and start wading toward others with smiles on their faces, while you feel tangled up and unable to interact? Maybe it's one of life's great mysteries that we'll never know. Or maybe it's just a little courage.

If you're not what you'd consider to be a very brave or outgoing person, there's a good chance that you're an introvert. Introverts have had a lot of publicity lately. A few years ago, it was considered a bad thing if you were given the label of introvert. Now, you come across many introverts through the Internet though you find extroverts as well. The truth is, you should be somewhere in the middle.

Introverts are people who enjoy seclusion and the quieter side of life. That doesn't mean you're relegated to that part of the world, but you probably do get scared off by social engagements and mixing with other people. If that's the case, don't worry. Around half the population is just like you and the other half is going to try and talk to you anyway.

One misconception about introverts is that they're automatically shy or have low self-esteem. Nothing can be farther from the truth. Some of my friends are introverts but they can confidently speak in front of thousands of people every week in church. Some of my introvert friends elicit the loudest of laughs and expressions of disbelief when they say that they are introverts. It's because they are able to hold their own in social gatherings and conversations. And like I said, some of them actually speak in front of thousands of people every weekend in church.

Being an introvert simply means your preference is solitude and silence. The difference that I see between my introvert and extrovert friends is that the introverts spend less time with other people, they get tired faster and go home earlier in most group nights out and are typically energized more by solitude than being around people. My extrovert friends spend more time with others, go home much later during group night outs and feel more energized when around people than when alone.

The point of all this is to tell you that what you're probably lacking is the desire and the bravery to actually approach someone and strike up a conversation with them. Now, the key to that is twofold. First, you need to get some courage and the second is that you need to get over yourself.

Courage and confidence are very closely tied together when it comes to speaking to other people. Bravery is what's going to get you into a situation, but confidence is what's going to get you to speak. For the sake of bravery, just do it. Going up to a person and talking to them or speaking up in a group is going to give you the chance to really flex your bravery. What you're facing is an anxiety wall when you're too scared to talk to others. By forcing yourself to overcome that anxiety once, you're going to make it easier for yourself to do it again and again. Eventually, it won't be scary anymore. I promise.

You can liken courage to your leg muscles – the more you train it, the stronger it becomes. One of my favorite forms of regular exercise is running. It hits so many birds with just one activity stone. It works out my heart, my lungs, my core muscles and my legs. When I first started, running past 1 kilometer felt like hell. I felt I'm gonna die from shortness of breath and the lactic acid build up in my legs made them feel like they're burning in hell. I could've sworn never to run again but due to insistent private demands, I continued running 3 times a week. Then a funny thing happened.

It became easier and easier and my running distances and speeds continued growing. My muscles, heart and lungs have started adapting to the increased stress it's subjected to when running and as a result, I became a stronger runner over time. It came to a point that running 10 kilometers was no big deal anymore.

It works pretty much the same way for your courage muscles. The more you practice doing something that scares the living daylights out of you, the easier it becomes, i.e., less daunting. Eventually, doing that thing that used to give you anxiety attacks will start to feel more natural and easy as breathing.

As for confidence, you're going to have to fake that one, in the beginning at least. Unless you're shaking and sweating a waterfall, people aren't going to know how scared you are. By pretending to be confident and ready for what you're about to say, you're going to come across as confident. By seeing that there's nothing to be afraid of, you'll feel that ease and comfort that comes with confidence. You'll think back and say: "It wasn't that bad." And you'll be absolutely right. So, I'm telling you to fake it until you make it when it comes to confidence.

Being a personable person is just about being friendly to others around you and having the courage and confidence to actually talk to them. If you approach any conversation with bravery and confidence, you're going to be able to talk to anyone. The ease and comfort you're looking for will come in time. I promise you that. Now, let's talk about how you do that effectively.

Ross Elkins

Chapter 3: The Confident Person

"Optimism is the faith that leads to achievement. Nothing can be done without hope and confidence." – Helen Keller

In the previous chapter, I mentioned the importance of confidence in being able to communicate effectively. Because all the best communications tips, tricks and strategies won't do much if you're not confident, we'll talk about confidence in more detail in this chapter. As I said, if courage is what gets you in the door (opportunity), it's confidence that will enable you to make the most inside that door (talk).

Confidence is like Floyd Mayweather – often misunderstood. In fact, it's so misunderstood that most people don't even want to be confident! Crazy, huh? But if you really want to master the art of effective interpersonal communications, then you shouldn't fear but embrace it instead. And the single biggest reason for such misconceptions are wrong mindsets. If you want to become confident, then you need to replace those old mindsets about confidence with new and accurate ones.

Why do you need to do that? The best way I can explain is through the illustration of wine in the Bible. Why the Bible? For one, this is where the principle I am about to explain to you is found. Second, the principle illustrated in the Bible about wine is no longer applicable today because of the newer and more efficient ways of producing and storing wine.

In the chapter XX verses of the book of XX in the Bible, Jesus Christ talked about mindsets in the context of wine and wineskins. He said you can't put new wine in old wineskins, which was the main way to store wine back in their day. Why? It's because the old wineskins won't be able to handle the new wine and it will burst.

The solution? Put new wine in new wine skins. The analogy I want to point here is that in the same vein, new ways of doing things (wine) cannot be contained in old wineskins (mindsets). You need to change your mind first before trying out new things.

Chapter 4: Identifying Old Confidence Mindsets

In order to make room for new wineskins (mindsets) to house the new wine (your new, confident self), you need to discard the old wineskins first. So what are the old wineskins you need to throw away. What are the old mindsets about confidence that are keeping you from pursuing it that you'll need to uproot?

Mindset #1: You Can Always Fake It

Yes, you probably heard it countless of times from others and in the media. You don't need to be legit – you can always fake it 'til you make it. No wonder there are lots of counterfeit items and people going around these days. Authenticity's no longer in style.

Some of these "fake it so you can make it" beliefs include acting like a millionaire so you'll attract positive energy that will eventually make you millions of dollars. Nothing else is as full of crap as that one. You don't act like a millionaire to be a millionaire. You work hard and smart to be one – or buy lottery tickets!

Think of it for a second here. Say you're as poor as a mouse and you hear some snake oil salesman preach this to you and for the sake of discussion, say you believed. If you're gonna act like a millionaire, where will you get the money to buy the things millionaires use and live the millionaire lifestyle? The only thing that is sure to happen is you're gonna get into debt and eventually, bankruptcy.

When it comes to being confident, it's not that acting like it – faking it as others would say – has no value. It has actually and it's not that it helps you deceive others into thinking that you're confident. Acting confident in the face of anxiety and self doubt can help make you feel confident from within, but the effect will be short-lived and shallow. Still it can help. For long-lasting self-confidence, however, you'll need to create a well inside you from which natural confidence continuously springs forth.

Counterfeit or temporary confidence will only help you convince half the people half the time. If I may add, you'll only be able to encourage yourself to be confident probably half the time too. Unless you develop a really deep, strong and true sense of confidence, your confident façade will fall down when challenges come your way.

The best way to go about this is to both change your mindset and your actions at the same time. Acting confident can give you a quick boost to encourage you in your efforts to renew your mind about yourself, which will make your initial acts of confidence become more and more natural, which continues an upward spiral to self-confidence.

It's OK to fake it in the beginning. Just don't put your hopes on it for long-lasting self-confidence.

Mindset #2: Confidence Is Hubris

Although hubris does involve self-confidence, it's much more than a healthy one. Hubris is being too confident in one's self, i.e., conceited, self-centered, feeling superior and arrogant. Just like all the other good things in life, too much confidence can be dangerous to your mental health.

Unfortunately, there's no gold standard, benchmark or magic number by which you can compare your own self-confidence. It also doesn't help that you can't measure yours objectively as well. That being said, how can you say if your confidence level is a healthy one or already in the general territory of hubris? You can get an idea if you're already way past the healthy self-confidence levels by looking at the following situations and your possible behavior:

-Interrupting: How can you say if interrupting someone who is talking hubris or confidence? If the person you're in a conversation with bad mouths your mother, calling her really degrading names and you cut him or her off to defend your mom's honor – that's confidence.

If on the other hand, you're with a group of friends and you interrupt the person who's excitedly sharing his or her successful attempt at landing a dream job just to interject your own personal story that's way off tangent, that's hubris.

- Pointing Fingers: If during a department meeting, you point your finger to your officemate who bypassed you in getting promoted to your desired position and genuinely telling him or her "You're the man/woman, man/woman!" with a sincere smile and tone of voice, that's confidence. Hubris is when you point your finger at someone when asking for a favor or asking them to do something for you.

-Dropping Name Bombs: Let's say you were in a party and you overhear the group next to you assassinating the character of your boss, who happens to be a very influential figure. Approaching the group to say, "I'm sorry but I personally know Mr. Influential figure and I beg to disagree with what you all are saying about him." is confidence.

On the other hand, if you cut in line to buy the latest iPhone model and tell the store clerk that "I'm friends with Steve (Jobs) and he said I don't need to fall in line." that's hubris and stupidity. Unless you have the uncanny ability to talk to the dead or you yourself are dead.

Mindset #3: Confidence Is Insensitivity

You don't need to step on other people's feelings and offend them to show you're confident. In fact, being insensitive to offending others' rights and beliefs isn't part of a healthy self-confidence.

Here are situations and contrasting potential responses to each that can help you get the idea between confidence and insensitivity:

-Smoking: Smoking – for as long as you do it legitimate smoking areas – is confidence, especially if smokers are normally vilified in your social circles. Smoking in non-smoking areas and turning down non-smokers' appeals for you to put out your cigarette is insensitivity and arrogance.

-Speaking Your Mind: When you're in a religious group of people who have a certain predisposition to a hotly contested moral issue and you are asked what your stand is concerning that hotly contested moral issue, confidence is respectfully telling them your position that's contrary to their group's. If on the other hand, you weren't asked and still you bluntly and disrespectfully tell them your dissenting opinion, that's insensitivity.

Mindset #4: Confidence Equals Chutzpah

Originally derived from the Hebrew or Jewish word hutspa, this word means audacity or insolence. As with hubris, chutzpah (pronounced as hutz-pah, silent "C") is another manifestation of excessive self-confidence.

So how can you tell if you're exhibiting hubris instead of confidence? Again, consider different reactions to the following situations to get an idea of what chutzpah is:

-Confidence is asking a Democrat to vote for a Republican or vice-versa. Chutzpah is mocking that person and telling him or her off if he or she declined your request.

-Confidence is asking the cafeteria lady for an extra serving of your favorite side dish. Chutzpah is asking for another extra serving to go.

-Confidence is asking the car double-parked in behind your car to move just enough so you can get out. Chutzpah is you double-parking behind a properly parked car and telling the driver to wait for you to finish withdrawing from an ATM kiosk with a long queue of people.

The Real Score With Confidence

Now that you've gotten the wrong mindsets about confidence out of the way and that you've cleared the path towards desiring to be self-confident for effective communications, it's time to look at what confidence really is about. Let's begin by looking at an orange tree.

If you plant an orange seed in your backyard, what do you honestly believe is the reasonable thing to happen? I bet we have the same answer: an orange tree will grow on that part of your background over time. In fact, you'd be very surprised – or scared – if you find an apple tree growing in that spot where you sowed orange seeds.

After so many years and the orange tree has fully matured, what fruit do you expect to harvest from it soon? That's right – oranges! It would be absurd and ridiculous to expect apples or lemons to grow on its branches, eh? But what about next season? Can you still expect to harvest the same? Of course, it's because it's an orange tree.

What if I cut off the branches and just retain the whole trunk? Can you still expect it to bear oranges within the next few seasons? Why, yes you can. Why is that so? For one, the tree is still alive and the branches will eventually grow back and once they do, you can expect the oranges to grow again.

But what if I cut the trunk and just leave the roots. Can you still expect to harvest oranges within the next couple of years? Yes you can for the same reason as when I cut the branches. The trunk will still grow back and eventually, so will the branches and fruits.

But what if after cutting the trunk, I also remove the roots from the ground. What then? Can you still expect oranges many years from now? Probably, but only if you plant another orange seed. But why did your answer change? It's because the roots are gone.

The same can be said about confidence. If your roots, i.e., your mindsets, are still against self-confidence, you can't expect to consistently act confident in the long run. Although acting confidently can help in the short-term, it'll be like grafting lemons on an orange trees to help you "enjoy" lemons from orange trees but the eventually, you'll won't be able to. It's because once you let up and stop grafting lemons onto it, the lemon fruits from the orange tree will stop as well. Acting confidently takes effort and if it doesn't become a natural part of you over time, you won't be able to sustain it.

On the other hand, if you're able to successfully plant and grow seeds of self-confidence in your subconscious mind, over time it will naturally bear fruits of confident behavior and speech, even if you don't try and think about it. It will just flow.

Thinking Your Way To Poverty – Or Out Of It

As much as I'd like the world to be free from any biases, it can be nothing more than wishful thinking. Why? It's because each and every one of us have different perspectives and values that were shaped by a million different life experiences. Because of such differences in experiences and personal circumstances, it's utterly impossible to achieve perfect harmony here on earth. Biases are here to stay and are as sure as death and taxes.

I'd like to compare two different people who came from the same backgrounds but ended up with totally different lives – Bernadette and Monisha – to illustrate how experiences can shape our beliefs and eventually our futures.

Bernadette is a 60-year old woman who lives in the slums of Metro Manila in the Philippines. She was born into a poor family from one of the country's far-flung provinces. She married at the young age of 18 years old and because of the folklore that riches can be easily had in the Metropolis, she and her husband migrated to Metro Manila within a year after being married. Thus they began their quest for their pot of gold.

Sadly, both of them never finished high school. Because of their lack of credentials, the only jobs they could find were menial – Bernadette worked as a household helper and her husband worked as a porter – people who carry passengers' luggage's at the country's premier shipping port. Both of them earn barely enough for their family's needs and their just one fever away from bankruptcy.

Bernadette believes this is her and her family's fate: they were born poor and they will die poor. Her faith in her God is strong but part of her faith – her mindset – is that it's God's will for her and her family to be poor and that to be holy means you should be poor, like Saint Francis and Mother Teresa. With those strong beliefs, they never sent their kids to school, even public ones that give poor children free education. What's the point, she thinks – they're fate is poverty anyway.

Contrast it with Monisha, who is also 60 years old and came from a poor family too. The difference is her grandparents who raised her instilled the value of a good education and the hope of getting out of poverty. She studied well in public school and was granted a scholarship in the country's premier public university, where she graduated with honors. And the rest was history – was hired as a management trainee straight from graduation, was sent to a prestigious international school for her master's degree and now, she sits on the board of one of the country's biggest companies.

Same background, same sad story but different endings. What made the difference?

Mindset. Bernadette's circumstances and life experiences worked together to give her a poverty-is-OK-and-holy mentality. Monisha's, on the other hand, were overridden by her grandparents' efforts at instilling in her the right mindsets of for being able to get out of poverty.

Mind Control

Yes, you don't have any control over the things that happen around you – the family you were born into, the neighborhood you grew up in, the economy you struggle in and the way people treat you. But here's one thing I know is true – that you can control your mind, particularly the way you think. And in particular, you can control or filter the things that enter your mind that can either help you or break you such as habits and attitudes.

Before going into the nitty-gritty, let me first explain how behavioral changes happen in general and how it applies to your desire to become confident. In particular, let me tell you about the conscious and subconscious mind.

The conscious mind is that part of your mind that you're aware of. It's responsible for all things that you intentionally do like moving your legs, deep breathing, composing an email and looking for your lost keys, among others. Your subconscious mind on the other hand, is that part of your mind that is responsible for coordinating and controlling many of your body processes such as your heartbeat, your normal breathing, your digestion and pulling your hand off a very hot plate as well as executing many movements that you no longer think about or focus on such as driving your car, playing the solo guitar part of Eric Clapton's Wonderful Tonight and swimming, among many others.

Imagine for a moment if you constantly need to focus and mentally process most of the things you need to do everyday, you'll go crazy! That's the reason why you and I have a subconscious mind – it takes care of those many, complicated things so you can focus on more urgent and important ones.

The conscious mind helps program many learned behaviors and skills into your subconscious mind. Remember one thing that you're very good at now that you used to struggle with at the beginning, such as driving your car or swimming? It wasn't natural for you at first, right? You always had to think about when to step on the clutch pedal, shift gears and the right and simultaneous timing of releasing the clutch and pushing the accelerator pedal to start the car moving from a dead stop. But after many hours of actual practice, especially on public roads, your conscious act of coordinating many movements eventually became so natural that you hardly think about the things you do while driving, right? In fact, you operate more on instinct now than intention. It means the skill has been successfully program from your conscious mind into your subconscious.

In the same manner, that's the general strategy for becoming a confident or a more confident person. You will do things using your conscious mind that will, over time, be successfully transferred and installed in your subconscious mind to make you a naturally confident person. You will no longer have to fake it because by that time, it's so natural that you will struggle trying to suppress it.

The best illustration I've ever read about how the conscious and subconscious minds work together to help us achieve our goals – including personal change – is from Dr. Maxwell Maltz' breakthrough book, PsychoCybernetics. In that book, Dr. Maltz likened the subconscious mind to a heat-seeking missile and the conscious mind as the pilot that gives the missile the target to seek out. The pilot can only program the target for the missile but as far as actually acquiring the target is concerned, it's all up to the missile. The missile is self-directed, meaning it makes the necessary adjustments if obstacles get in the way or if the target moves to a new location.

The subconscious mind is like that. It works best unsupervised and uncontrolled because it has its own mind. The best way to utilize it is to give it suggestions and commands as to what goals to pursue then let it be. So if you want to be a confident person, you can use your conscious mind to "program" your subconscious mind into making you a truly confident person.

This will explain why when you try so hard to change yourself or learn something, it seems to backfire and you end up failing and frustrated. This also explains why many breakthroughs seem to happen "out of the blue" when we least expect it, when we're relaxed. It's because the subconscious mind has been fully programmed at that point and is able to operate – seek the goal target – unimpeded like the heat seeking missile. When we try so hard, we use our conscious mind and in so doing, we tend to impede the work of the subconscious.

The question now is – do you want to become naturally confident and as a result, become a very effective communicator? If so, let's look at how you can re-program your subconscious mind to make you a truly confident person that will be able to really maximize the techniques you'll learn to become an effective communicator.

Ross Elkins

Chapter 5: Uprooting Old Mindsets

The next step after identifying your old limiting mindsets about being a confident person is removing them or uprooting them to make space for new, empowering ones. How do you do that? Here are some of the most practical ways you can do so.

Hang Out With Confident Communicators

There's a saying that birds of the same feather flock together. The principle behind it is that we all tend to be drawn to those who are most like us in terms of personality, interests or needs, among others. But I have a different take on this tried and tested statement.

I believe that as you hang out more and more with the kinds of people that you want to be, the more your existing mindsets about confidence are eroded because you yourself get to see the opposite of what you believe in. Take for example, the wrong mindset that confidence is hubris. When you get to hangout with really confident people and personally witness that confidence and humility can actually co-exist, your old mindset starts to be uprooted and over time, you're able to ditch it.

<u>Doubt Your Belief</u>

Another way to uproot or demolish old limiting mindsets is to constantly question their validity. It's like slowly chipping away at a big and formidable wall. Over time and with enough "chipping", the wall crumbles down.

Imagine if you will a courtroom drama like Law And Order or the classic show L.A. Law. During hearings, you will notice that the main job of the defense attorney is to establish reasonable doubt on the prosecution's evidences and accusations. How does the defense do this? By questioning the validity of the evidences and claims presented by the prosecution.

It pretty much works the same way for your subconscious mind. You can do this by asking questions that cast reasonable doubt on your existing limiting belief or mindsets about our confidence such as:

"How much of this mindset is true? Is there even any tinge of truth to this at all? Why is it that some of the most confident people I know are actually not insensitive or rude to others?"

"Will holding on to this mindset be good or bad for me? Will letting go of this mindset harm me or help me? Will I this mindset bring me closer to becoming an effective communicator or not?"

Ask it often and soon, you'll find yourself doubting such mindsets and eventually uproot them fully.

Starve Your Enemy

One sure way to kill a formidable enemy, regardless of your size or strength, is to starve him to death. It may take a longer time than most other ways of killing him but the result is sure – victory! Since your current limiting mindsets about confidence are formidable enemies, it is therefore a good idea to starve them to death.

To be able to better understand how to starve your limiting mindsets to death, it's better that you first realize how you're actually feeding them. One of the ways you unconsciously do that is by meditating on it. Now, you may think you're not guilty of it because you don't sit on the floor in what's known as the lotus position and chant "ohmmmm" and "ahhmmmm" for hours on end. Meditation simply means to think about something many times over on a regular basis. So when you look at it, daydreaming is a kind of meditation as well.

Whenever you think about how hard it would be to work on your self-confidence and become an effective communicator, you're meditating on why you won't be a confident and effective communicator. You're feeding the enemy that way. You're making stronger and bigger.

Now you know how you feed it, how do you practically starve it? You simply stop meditating about it! If meditating on your limiting confidence mindsets feeds them even more, then not meditating on or thinking about it is starving those enemies to death. No, you don't deny such thoughts...you simply acknowledge it and move on – just let it slide. Then replace it by meditating on your new and empowering confidence mindsets.

Chapter 6: New Mindsets For Confidence

Now that you've identified the wrong mindsets that keep you from becoming and staying confident as well as how to uproot them from your subconscious mind, it's time to identify the right ones that will help you start becoming confident.

The Confidence- Achievement-Confidence Cycle

The best way to become confident is to have something concrete to be confident about, i.e., achievements, personal traits and characteristics. However, it isn't necessary that you start from there. What if realistically speaking, you don't have anything concrete to be proud of? Does it mean you're doomed to a life with little or no confidence in yourself? I beg to disagree.

You can start by building some level of confidence that'll be enough to help you move forward and achieve small successes. Those small victories will make you more confident to take on bigger things and bigger successes. It becomes an upward cycle that will continue increasing your achievements and confidence.

You can start by thinking yourself confident, then act confident and eventually be confident.

Changeable

You need to realize and really believe in your subconscious mind that your life isn't fixed, like what Bernadette believed about her and her family's lifelong poverty sentence. Your beliefs, your personality, your character and your life can change and you can do something to make that happen. You have the power to change those things and your life.

I don't mean to be rude or insensitive but some of the silliest and most debilitating mindsets I've ever come across with include the following:

"This is the mold in which God fashioned me and hence, this mold is fixed for life."

"My parents weren't entrepreneurs and none from my clan are either so I can't be an entrepreneur."

"I've always been shy since I was a kid and that's how I'll be for life, I guess."

"I've never succeeded at anything worthwhile in the past, so what makes me think I can do any differently forever?"

These statements are the best examples of truly confidence-destroying mindsets that a person can have if they don't learn to control their minds. It can happen to you too if you do the same. Statements like these work two ways to keep you from succeeding. It makes light of whatever accomplishments you may have had in the past and it robs you of hope.

Yes, there are things that are beyond your control but that shouldn't mean you should give up on those that you have control over – those that are within your circle of influence. You have to have faith that your current status in life, personality and mind aren't permanent and that you can change it. And the moment you're able to change them, you'll start to feel true confidence oozing out from you – a naturally easy confidence that sticks and isn't fleeting.

Excellence

True and lasting confidence is grounded on excellence, not perfection. Believing that confidence requires perfection is a sure fire way for your confidence to leak out constantly. In fact, you may never even have any semblance of self-confidence if you're aiming for perfection instead of excellence.

Excellence is giving it your all, exceeding standards consistently and giving great quality results. I don't know about you but those are realistically achievable goals! Remember, you need actual accomplishments for you to have any hope of enjoying a strong and lasting self-confidence. If you're not able to achieve anything, you won't just stagnate – you'll also descend into a state of low self-esteem over time.

Perfection is an impossible dream. If you make impossible dreams your goals, you're sure to not achieve anything. Without achievements, you'll have no hope of ever enjoying a long-lasting sense of confidence. That's why believe you can be excellent, not perfect.

To help encourage you that excellence is the bedrock of self-confidence and not perfection, I'd like for you to take a look at 3 of the most accomplished and confident people in the planet: Stephen Curry, Manny Pacquiao and Cristiano Ronaldo. These three athletes are some of the best their respective sports have ever seen. But as much as their mega accomplishments have made them famous, another thing they have in common aside from oozing confidence in themselves and in their ability to perform at the highest levels of their respective sports is that they all have "misses" in their stats. Stephen Curry may make most of his shots from any possible angle on the court but he still misses some. Manny Pacquiao may be the only professional boxer in history to dominate 8 different weight classes but he has suffered defeats in his entire professional boxing career.

And Cristiano Ronaldo too, like Stephen Curry, isn't always able to successfully kick the soccer ball into the goal – he misses too.

They're all not perfect but they're all excellent in their respective fields of sports. And that's what confidence is about.

Ross Elkins

Chapter 7: Installing The New Program – Empowering Confidence Mindsets

"Your mind is a garden. Your thoughts are the seeds. You can grow flowers or you can grow weeds." – Ritu Ghatourey

After identifying and uprooting limiting confidence mindsets and coming up with new and empowering ones, it's time to install those new "programs" into your subconscious mind for implementation. If your question includes how do you do that, then here are the answers.

Affirmations

Your thoughts can be likened to your physical muscles in the sense that they can be exercised for increased strength or flexibility. And as such, you can also reduce heir strength and flexibility by not using them. The reduction in muscle size and strength due to reduced or total inability to use them regularly is called atrophy.

Your mind can also suffer from atrophy when you don't use it often like your physical muscles. That's why experts highly recommend challenging puzzles for senior citizens like crossword puzzles and Sudoku as a way of slowing down the deterioration of their mental faculties.

Positive affirmations – also known as positive self-talk – are a good way to keep your thoughts actively exercised and helps you build up confidence. Also, it's one of the best ways to reprogram your subconscious mind into acquiring a new target – self confidence. Use it or lose it, it's up to you.

Of course you'll ask me how does one actually or practically utilize positive affirmations to experience long lasting life change. Here's how to do it:

-Take a piece of paper (preferably A4 sized) and fold it lengthwise in half. On one side, write all the limiting confidence mindsets you identified and would want to uproot.

-On the other side, write down all the new and empowering confidence mindsets you'd like to replace the limiting ones with.

-When done with both sides, tear the paper in half along the folded line and throw away the side that contains the old, limiting confidence mindsets.

-Make several copies of the side that contains the new and empowering mindsets and post them on all the areas of your home that you frequent and keep one copy in your wallet so you can frequently see and read them.

-For optimal results, read them aloud whenever time permits. It's different when you hear them instead of just reading them silently.

-Even when you feel you've already reached that point wherein you're confident enough to be an effective communicator, I strongly encourage you to continue with it. Better err on the side of caution than of error. By keeping it up, you minimize the chances of old, banished limiting confidence mindsets creeping back in and making a garden in your subconscious mind.

Hang Out With Confident Communicators – The Return

Yes, hanging out with such people don't just help in uprooting old mindsets. It also helps you instill new ones simply by impartation and witnessing. In fact, as you witness and absorb their confident ways, you unconsciously ease out the old, limiting confidence mindsets until they're fully uprooted and replaced by new, empowering ones. Just keep in mind that more is caught than taught and in this regard, hanging out helps you catch more confidence.

Take The Leap

If you wait for things to be perfect – for all your ducks to be in a row – before doing anything to help you become a confident and effective communicator, you'll never move. Procrastination is a very real threat here.

Acting on what you learned is one of the best ways to make your learning trickle down to the subconscious from your conscious mind. Constant application and practice buries those skills and actions even further into your subconscious mind and eventually, program it there for a natural and effortless confidence. This is why top athletes like Stephen Curry, Manny Pacquiao and Cristiano Ronaldo continue practicing their skills even if they're already at the top of their respective sports.

Chapter 8: Interpersonal

When you break down communication to its core, it's going to bring down all other forms of communication to interpersonal. So what is interpersonal? It's the communication between two people and that's it. Eventually, you just break it down so that two people are talking to each other and that's what I'm going to talk about in this chapter. Here you go.

When you're communicating with others, you're going to want to make sure that you're aware what's going on. One on one communication is how most of us establish friendships and relationships that last for years to come. It's a process that most people begin when they're children but over time they can develop anxiety and fears about the process that really starts to hinder them.

What you need to do is remember that you're talking with another person who isn't judging you. Most people are open and receptive to others when they're approached and those people are only going to judge you if you're awkward. So, if you're looking to give your interpersonal communication an extra boost, here are some tips to help you establish yourself as a communicator.

Ask Questions:

I mean this in the least self-centered or judgmental way possible: people love talking about themselves. If you don't ask questions, you're not giving people a chance to really tell you who they are, what they've done, or how they feel about things. Instead of dominating the conversation or letting dead air rise, just ask them some questions and give them a chance to talk.

Asking questions have another benefit that makes you a much more effective communicator: knowledge of the other person. The more you ask about them, the more you know about them and the more you do, the more you'll know how best to communicate with them so that they can really understand your message, avoid misinterpretations and increase the chances of you eliciting your desired responses or reactions.

Eye Contact:

While too much eye contact makes people uncomfortable, a healthy amount really inspires a sense of trust and connection between two people. Actually look them in the eye when you're talking to them and don't be afraid of giving them that extra special commitment during a conversation. People like to feel like they're the focus of the person they're with.

When you're able to employ proper eye contact to the person your talking to, you make them feel good about themselves, which makes them feel good about you, of course. As such, they become more open to whatever it is you're communicating and as a result, you may easily be able to elicit your desired responses or reactions to the messages you're transmitting.

Get Rid of Your Phone:

When you're in a one on one situation with another person and you have your cell phone out or you're checking it, you're sending a clear and cruel message. It says you're not that important to me. By checking your phone or having it on, you're doing more damage than you could ever hope to repair. Stop being so attached to your phone and put it away if you really want to build a relationship with someone.

Remember, if you want to be an effective communicator, you have to make the person you're communicating to feel really comfortable with you and like you. Making them feel you're genuinely interested in them by giving them your full attention is a sure fire way of making them feel that way about you. When you ditch your phone, you minimize your risk of ruining whatever rapport you may have already established by being distracted and make the other person feel not so special.

Engage:

When you're talking with someone, don't just stare at him or her blankly. Nodding your head, asking questions, giving these subtle hints that you're paying attention to what they're saying is a great way to draw someone closer and make them feel like you've really invested in them.

This is where body language, gestures and facial expressions come into play. They can – in very subtle ways – tell the other person that you're interested in them, that they're important and that they matter. Again, when you make the other person feel good about themselves, you make them like you and when that happens, they become more and more open to what you're communicating.

When it comes to interpersonal relationships, it's time to get serious about them. If you want a relationship with someone, then you need to put the time and energy into actually building up that relationship. By simply enacting these very basic and reasonable skills, you're going to find that people think you're a much more engaging, genuine person. After all, that's what you want in the end. So start implementing these changes right now.

Communication

Ross Elkins

Chapter 9: Non-Verbal Communication

According to Martha Graham, the body never lies. I believe that. As effective communications is about 90% non-verbal and only 10% verbal, non-verbal communications can make or break what you're verbally trying to communicate.

When interacting with other people, you send and receive very subtle signals that you may not be aware of. Your actions like the way you stand up, sit and look at the person your interacting with transmits messages that you, in your conscious mind, are unable to detect or recognize.

The problem often lies when what you say doesn't seem to match with what you're not trying to say – your non-verbal communications. Because action speaks louder than words, most people will choose to side with your actions (non-verbals) instead of what you're verbally saying. In most cases, this side choosing is brought about by a sense that something's "off" or not right.

One example of this is – and I don't mean to offend – sales people. Often times, I just know when all they see when they look at me is a big, fat $ sign even if they say all the right things and execute their scripted spiels perfectly without batting an eyelash. I can't put a handle on it but I just feel something's off and that they' aren't sincere. Many times, I'm proven right as they don't bother to call me after I said "I'll think about it – give me a ring next week."

How you react, listen, move your body and look at the other person tells the person if you're sincere or not. When you're able to master non-verbal communication, you have a very powerful weapon that can give your words more influence and power but if you're not able to, it can be a weapon that cuts your own hand.

So how does non-verbal communications assist you in effectively sending your message to the other party? First, it does so by practically repeating what you said in a non-verbal way. If you tell your interviewer for a certain position that you're the best person for the job, the way you stand, gesture and establish eye contact can subtly and silently repeat and reinforce what you said about you being the best candidate for the job.

Aside from subtle repetition of what you say, non-verbal communications assist you in getting your messages across by supplementing your verbal messages. A good example of this is mourning with a friend over the loss of a loved one. When you go the wake and you see your friend, your act of hugging her for an extended period of time and crying greatly reinforces your verbal condolences. Another example would be embracing a dear friend whom you have missed dearly because you haven't seen him in a long while. When you tell that friend you missed him so much, your embrace solidifies that statement of yours and makes him feel that you really did miss him a lot.

Non-verbal communications can also enable you to effectively communicate your message by taking the place of words. An example of this would be the body language of people who just lost someone whom they love very much. As they mourn, their posture, gestures and facial expressions are dead giveaways or signs that say, "Hey, I'm mourning. Please mourn with me!" even without that person saying anything. If a picture paints a thousand words, then non-verbal communications paint several pictures.

Setting Up Your Effectively Powerful Non-Verbal Communications

Non-verbal communications can be thought of as a reciprocal and fast-moving process, which requires attention and focus. If you don't, you run the risk of missing out on very subtle but important details due to day dreaming or getting distracted by an external stimuli. Those details can make or break you efforts to communicate effectively. That's why part of preparing yourself for using non-verbal communications powerfully and effectively is to focus and pay attention to the other person.

Another way to prepare yourself for non-verbal communications is by managing your stress well. You may be asking yourself, what does that have to do with effectively communicating without words? Well, a lot. For starters, stress can cause you to act in a totally opposite way from what you're trying hard to communicate. For example, if you're saying all the right things at the right time to someone you're interested dating but due to stress and lack of sleep, you yawn and sometimes jerk your head as you fight the urge to fall asleep, you subtly send the signal that he or she's not interesting enough, even if that's not true. Second, if you're so stressed out, it will show in your facial expression. If you're trying to convince a prospective client that your company's product is the best in the market but your facial expression's somewhat flat because of lack of sleep, the client will pick up on your facial expression during presentation and feel something's "off" with what you're saying.

Your inability to manage your stress levels well can also lead to somewhat agitated body language, e.g., look angry or displeased, even if you're not. It may send the message that you are agitated or displeased with the other party even if your words – and sincere intention – say you appreciate and honor them.

Being aware of how you feel is another good way to prepare for effective non-verbal communications. When you are, then you can consciously alter your body language so it'll be consistent with what you're trying to say. If you're aware that you're feeling dejected and you're about to give an inspirational message to a graduating class, you have the power to straighten up your body, look straight, smile and gesture wildly to impart the message with passion and credibility.

It's not just your emotions that you should be aware of - you should also be aware of the other party's. When you are, you'll be able to figure out the best channel of communications to use for effectively sending your message across. If for example, you noticed that the other party's sad, you'll consciously avoid any body language that seems to be insensitively perky. That way, you can engage the other person well, connect and be able to communicate effectively with him or her.

In the next chapter, we'll look at the primary way non-verbal communications are done: body language.

Ross Elkins

Chapter 10: Body Language

Body language and non-verbal communications are as inseparable as Batman and Robin and Hall and Oates. Basically, non-verbal communications is primarily about body language. And speaking of, while it's true that you can purposefully use it to communicate status, personality and confidence even if you feel otherwise, you can't do it for long. Why? Because eventually, how you really feel about yourself will come out. This is why I placed confidence before non-verbal communication or body language: confidence is the foundation that enables you to consistently employ body language for effective communications.

Body language enables you to develop confidence but only to a certain degree and if you don't build it up from within, your body language will eventually find you out. But regardless if you're already confident or are still working on it, knowing how the following body language expressions can help you become an effective communicator a.s.a.p. Just remember to continue working on your confidence.

Facial Expressions

The face can be a very effective channel by which you can send messages to another person. It's so effective that facial expressions have spawned a field of study dedicated to reading them accurately. If you want to know more just good are your facial expressions in communicating messages, watch several episodes of the TV series Lie To Me starring Tim Roth. Tim plays the lead character Dr. Cal Lightman, who heads the Lightman group, which is a company who specializes in reading facial expressions and determines if people are lying or not. It's somewhat based on the life and exploits of leading facial reading expert Dr. Paul Ekman, who works with the various clients – the government included – to determine if people are telling the truth and in the process, help solve crimes.

Body Movements And Posture

Have you ever gotten strong impressions about people after seeing them sit, stand or walk the way the do? If you have, then you would agree with me that their posture and actions help shape the way you see them, right? It's the same with others when you communicate to them. They unconsciously observe your body movements and posture. The way you stand can give away how you truly see yourself (confident or unconfident) and your walk may suggest if you're an alpha male or not.

Gestures

Often times, small movements are taken for granted. However, they carry more weight than most people – or you for that matter – assign to them. Gestures like waving and pointing your fingers can speak loudly about who you are as a person and how you truly look at things and people. One thing about gestures though is that the interpretations of such vary from one culture to another. This is why one of the most important things you should prepare for when going to another country for the first time is their culture so you can minimize the risk of erroneously gesturing something they'd consider as taboo or socially unacceptable.

Touch

Like gestures, this is also often taken for granted and are also subtly powerful communicators of what's really going on inside of us. Consider the last time you shook hands with someone who was just introduced to you. What impressions did you get about the other person based on their handshake, e.g., a strong person or a weak one? Or what about the last time your mom hugged you after not seeing you for months on end – how'd that feel and can you sense her excitement about seeing you and how much she misses you?

Space

Have you ever experienced talking to another person who is so close to you that it felt like the two of you were already exchanging oxygen and carbon dioxide? Did it feel uncomfortable because it seemed like they were invading your private space?

Have you ever been in a situation where you spoke to a loved one whom you missed so much only to notice that they seem to be keeping a rather far distance from you? How'd that feel? Did it seem like things weren't OK between the both of you?

Physical space can communicate how the person is feeling about you, e.g., too comfortable or too aloof. It can also communicate how you feel about the other person. If done correctly, you can subtly send messages of affection, intimacy, aggression or dominance.

Touch

Touch can subtly communicate to the other person how confident or unconfident you are. For example, a firm handshake is a sign of confidence while a weak one is a sign of low self-esteem. A strong hug may indicate that you missed the person very much while a weak one may mean you didn't.

Voice

There's a saying that you can be right but wrong at the top of your voice. Simply put, the tone of your voice can either invalidate or support what you just said. If I apologized to you but my tone of voice is more mocking than penitent, which between my words and my tone of voice would you believe? Your tone of voice can send subtle messages of affection, confidence, sarcasm or anger.

Ross Elkins

Chapter 11: Influence

When we're communicating with people around us, we want to be able to influence them. Influence is much better than power because once you step down from it or you're no longer powerful, they won't listen to or follow you anymore. However, when you are able to influence them, you don't have to lift a finger or worry about them listening to you and acting on your message because influence makes them want to do it.

Persuasion is one of the most important skills in the business world and in our lives in general. The ability to take people who are in no camp or in the opposite camp and bring them over to your way of thinking is something that will help you for years to come. So how are you going to be able to get people to be influenced by you right now? What steps do you need to take to make a difference?

Well, the first thing I would suggest to you is to know where you stand on situations. Before I give you any tips for you daily interactions, I want you to take a day and really examine who you are. If you don't know what it is you believe in or what it is you stand for, then it's going to be hard to ever get someone to stand with you. Remember that all influence and persuasion is about tying whatever it is you're talking about to a value or a human desire in your life. Know what it is you stand for and find a way to make that come out through your communication.

After you've done your soul searching, go ahead and implement the following steps into getting people to be influenced and inspired by who you are and what it is you're trying to do.

Believe in it:

Whatever you're trying to inspire in people, you need to believe in it or find some way to actually and truly commit to it. If the people around you are not seeing your one hundred percent dedication to the cause, then they're not going to follow you into the dark. Having a true heart and a true dedication to what it is you're working on is going to get other people to believe in it as well.

Light the Fires:

Passion is the single most important attribute that you're going to need when it comes to inspiring people and gaining influence. Look at cult leaders if you need any more evidence. By having passion, you spark and ignite it in everyone around you and people are desperately looking for that fire as well. So find what you're passionate about and let it inject the power and the drive inside of every aspect of your life. People will be drawn to it and they will want to be part of what you're doing.

Be a Stand up Soul:

The fastest way to get people to not like you and not want to be influenced by you is to have a moral character that questionable, shady or malign. People want to feel like they're doing the right thing and are on the right side, so make it your goal to be the best you can be. It's time to be an adult and make the right and best decisions that you can. All eyes are on you and you should start acting that way. No more questionable decisions.

Have Value:

If you want to be influential, you need to have value. That's the most important thing when it comes to influence. If you have position, authority, resources or character, people are going to give ear to what you say. If you're at the bottom of the pyramid, it's going to be hard to gain that influence and that respect that you desire. So, get out there and find some value to who you are. With hard work and a little cunning, you can decipher where you stand in the world and why people want to listen to you.

Influence is something that we all want to have. Everyone wants to feel like they have something worth saying and we want people to listen to us. So when you're looking to see what it is you have worth influencing people over, make sure that you use it for the good of humanity and make people want to rally behind you. After all, everyone wants to be in the good guy's corner.

Chapter 12: Social Skills

For many people, social skills are something that died in college, or unfortunately never developed fully in the first place. If you're not sure what social skills are, then you have my condolences. However, we're going to rectify those problems immediately and have you acting like a social expert.

A quick refresher on the subject. Social skills are communication dynamics and abilities that help you in social environments. So, what skills do you have that are going to help you out when you're in large groups of people? For some of us, we immediately switch over into one of two archetypes of the party scene: obnoxious partygoer or reclusive gargoyle. You don't want to be either of those. You want to have sufficient presence to make people listen to you and acknowledge you.

So here are several suggestions I have for you to implement right away in getting people to take you seriously at the next party.

Not the Sun:

You are not the beaming light of the party, unless this is a birthday party or a celebration just for you. At the average event and party, you don't want to be the loudest, most talkative person in the room. In fact, you want to strike a nice balance of engaging with people and letting them engage with you. Don't be the center of attention. You need to be an accent to the party.

Putting the spotlight on yourself is one of the best ways to turn people away. Nobody likes a pompous, self-centered person. One of the basic human relations principles is that people like people who like them and by trying to put the spotlight on you means you're not interested about them – you're more concerned about glorifying yourself instead. If that's the case, then no one will be interested enough to like you.

Not the Shade:

That being said, you don't want to be silently walking around avoiding people. Go up to people that you know and start talking to them. No one wants to cling to the person they know, so be willing to step away. Look at other people alone or standing by themselves and approach them to talk. They'll be more than willing to have a word with a new, friendly face. Just don't be a shadow through all of this.

While trying to be the center of attention isn't good and can backfire on you socially, the other extreme of being a wallflower is equally bad. If you keep quiet and simply blend in with the environment, people won't notice you. If they don't notice you, then how can you effectively communicate with them? The key here is moderation. There's a fine line between trying to grab attention to yourself and making social contact with people.

Engage Everyone:

When you're in a group of people talking, there's usually one person who isn't saying much. If you have one of these quiet vortexes in your group, they're probably one of two things. The first is that they're shy and want to be part of the conversation. So talk to them. Ask them their opinion and get them talking. You'll make a new friend and hear something new. The second option is that the person not talking is probably the smartest person in the group. A smart person talks less than he listens and you're going to want to hear what they have to say.

Either way, engaging everyone in a naturally interested in them way can only be good for you socially speaking. Why? First of all, it indicates you aren't a social snob and that you're an inclusive type of person that anyone can feel comfortable with. Second, it speaks of quiet but strong confidence in yourself because by engaging everyone as much as possible, it shows you aren't intimidated by social status. So go ahead and be a social butterfly. In this case, it isn't bad to be so.

Chivalry is Not Dead:

Nor is it gender specific. Having good manners and proper etiquette is the best way to make people respect you and feel like you're a person worth listening to. By being willing to be an upstanding person, you're making it easier for people to want to hear what you're saying. So take a chance and be an upstanding person of great moral character. It'll pay off in spades at a social event for you.

Chivalry, if played right, speaks highly of you. First, it sends the message that you are an educated and cultured person. Second, it sends the message that you're one of a kind. I remember recently when a female friend of mine noticed how I always walk on the outer most side of the curb when with a female companion and told me how she appreciated that very much because it seems chivalry is dead – I'm the only person she knows who still does it. And when you make the other person feel good about themselves, they'll like you as a result. And that breaks down a big chunk of the effective communications barrier.

Social skills are difficult for a lot of people who have let them get rusty or have abandoned them all together. So take some time to brush up on what it means to have social skills in an actual social situation. It's worth taking the time to brush up so that you're not making a fool of yourself in front of everyone.

Ross Elkins

Chapter 13: Listening

Diverse circumstances oblige distinctive sorts of tuning in. We may listen to acquire data, enhance a connection, pick up gratefulness for something, make discriminations, or participate in a discriminating assessment. Regardless of the intention, mastering the art of listening is one of the best ways to become an effective communicator.

Most people have the impression that effective communications is one way, i.e., from them to the other person. As such, most people tend to interrupt, reassure, advise, analyze, judge, argue, criticize, threaten, moralize, diagnose, divert, etc. However, excellent or effective communications require the ability to listen well aside from merely being able to talk. Maybe that's why we have 2 ears and one mouth; so we can listen twice more than we should speak. The sad part is that most people are trained only in the art of speaking and not in terms of listening.

Paying attention is the very first step in becoming a very good listener. And to be a good listener doesn't mean just passive listening but actively doing so. Consider this: how do you feel when the person you're talking to isn't paying attention to you?

You'll probably feel frustrated, annoyed, rejected, discounted, angry or anxious, among others. When you feel that way, doesn't it become harder for you to really get what the other person is saying? Now try being on the other side. How do you think will your ability to effectively communicate be affected if you don't actively listen to the person you're speaking to?

While certain aptitudes are essential and fundamental for different kinds of tuning in (the processes of receiving, attending, and understanding), every sort obliges some extraordinary abilities.

Different types of Listening

1. ***Analytical Listening***

The capacity to listen analytically is a key in a vote based system. At work, in the group, at administration clubs, in places of love, in the family—there is for all intents and purposes no spot you can go where listening analytically is immaterial.

Government officials, the media, business people, promoters of arrangements and strategies, and our own money related, enthusiastic, scholarly, physical, and otherworldly needs oblige us to place a premium on analytic listening and the reasoning that goes with it.

The subject of this type of listening merits significantly more consideration than we can bear the cost of it here. Be that as it may, there are three things to remember. These three things were delineated by Aristotle, as we all know, the great traditional Greek rhetorician, more than thousands of years ago prior in his treatise, The Rhetoric. Those important three things are: ethos, or speaker validity; logos, or intelligent contentions; what's more, pathos, or mental offers. .

a.   *Ethos*

Validity of the speaker is imperative. The two basic components of speaker validity are expertness what's more, reliability. A speaker may be master or competent enough yet still not to be considered dependable. Case in point, a totalitarian despot of a certain underdeveloped nation may be a master on the topic of his nation's ownership of atomic arms; yet I would not believe him to let me know. On the other hand a man may be dependable, yet not be a master on the subject. I believe my closest companion; he would tell me reality about atomic arms in that underdeveloped nation, in the event that he knew and I asked him. In any case, his data would be of sketchy legitimacy since he is not a master of such things but only a simple person.

At the point when listening to a message that obliges a basic judgment or reaction, ask yourself, "Is the speaker a valid source, one who is both a specialist on the subject furthermore, one who can be trusted to be completely forthright, impartial, and clear?" Remember that a man may have identity or magnetism. Be that as it may, these don't take the spot of believability. A man may even be profoundly able and a specialist in one zone and basically not be educated in another.

Successful analytical listening requires watchful judgment about the expertness and dependability of the speaker.

Truth be told, ethos or speaker believability may be the most essential single element in basic listening and considering.

In any case, ethos without logos is insufficient.

b.   *Logos*

Indeed, even speakers with high ethos frequently make mistakes in rationale, not by expectation, but rather unintentionally, imprudence, negligence to detail, or absence of examination. Discriminating audience members have a privilege to expect very much upheld contentions from speakers, contentions that contain both genuine recommendations and legitimate inductions or conclusions.

At the point when assessing contentions, audience members ought to pose a few questions about the recommendation or articulations made:

- Are the announcements genuine?

- Are the information worthwhile to be known?

- Are the sources of the information known to the audience members?

As such do audience members know where the data originated from?

- Is the information precisely depicted?

  - Is the information delegate? That is, would all the information, or if nothing else a prevalence of it demonstrate the same thing?

The above inquiries might all be offered an explanation as to your sake, yet the rationale may be flawed. For maybe the information will try not to prompt or legitimize the surmising or conclusions drawn. Audience members ought to ask themselves the accompanying questions:

  - Is the determination a hundred % sure or are special cases conceivable?

  - Were all reason impact connections built up certain?

- Does the information legitimize the derivation reached or the inference given?

- Does the derivation or conclusion "take after" from the information

- Arrives proof of solid sensible speculation by the speaker?

Both ethos and logos are vital components of discriminating tuning in. However, dependence on simply these two components without a thought of sentiment would be like trying to sit on a three-legged stool with one leg missing. This third leg is *Pathos*.

c.   *Pathos*

The mental or passionate component of correspondence is frequently misjudged and abused.

Basically said, speakers frequently utilize mental appeals to pick up a passionate reaction from audience members. Powerful discriminating audience members painstakingly focus on the center of the speaker's message.

Speakers may engage any one or a few needs, cravings, or qualities that are critical to us including: experience, thrift, interest, dread, innovativeness, fellowship, blame, autonomy, dedication, force, pride, sensitivity, selflessness. There are numerous others, obviously; the rundown is a long one.

There are a few inquiries discriminating audience members ought to inquire themselves when evaluating the *Pathos* component:

- Is the speaker endeavoring to control as opposed to induce me?

- What is the speaker's real intention?

- Does he (the speaker) know how to combine pathos and logos?

- Am I only focusing and reacting just to *pathos*?

- One week from now or one year from now will I be fulfilled by the choice I am making today?

Compelling analytical listening relies on upon the audience keeping every one of the three components of the message in the investigation and in context: ethos, or source validity; logos, or coherent contention; and pathos, or mental claim.

2.   ***Appreciative Listening***

Appreciative listening incorporates listening to music for happiness, to speakers on the grounds that you like their speaking style, to your decisions in theatre, TV, radio, or film. It is the reaction of the audience, not the origin of the message that characterizes this type of listening. One that suggests appreciative listening for one individual may give something else for another. The nature of this particular type of listening depends in huge part on three variables: presentation, recognition, and past experiences.

a.   *Presentation*

Presentation incorporates numerous components: the medium, the setting, the style and identity of the moderator, to name only a couple. Once in a while it is our view of the presentation, as opposed to the actual and real presentation, that most impacts our listening joy or dismay. Perception is a vital component in appreciative listening.

b.   *Recognition*

Having expectations assume an extensive part in recognition. Recognitions—and the desires that drive them—have their premise in states of mind. Our states of mind decide how we respond to, and cooperate with, our general surroundings. Absolutely, they are essential determinants with reference to regardless of whether we appreciate or welcome the things we listen to. Clearly, recognitions additionally figure out what we listen to in the first place.

c.   *Past experience*

When we talk about the process of perception it is somehow clear that past experience impacts whether we appreciate listening to something. At times, we appreciate listening to things in light of the fact that we are specialists in the range. In some cases, then again, mastery or past experience keeps us from getting a charge out of a presentation on the grounds that we are excessively delicate, making it impossible to defects. Past experience assumes an expansive part in grateful tuning in.

Numerous individuals appreciate the hints of expansive city activity. Perhaps their childhood was spent in a huge city and it was a considerable cheerful experience for them. The boom of horns blaring, the sound of thundering motors quickening, even the ear-splitting yell of sirens penetrating the air—every one of these things may help them to remember lovely times in their lives. They acknowledge hearing these sounds.

Others, having experienced childhood with a homestead or in a residential area, have figured out how to appreciate the hints of nature. For them, a stroll in the small village produces hints of satisfaction: the stir of leaves in the breeze, the melody of a robin, the jibber jabber of a rivulet.

For the most part, on the off chance that we relate a sound or other involvement with lovely recollections, then we acknowledge or appreciate it. Be that as it may, in the event that the sound or experience is connected with unpalatable recollections, we likely won't acknowledge or appreciate it.

However, we can transform, we ought not to close our brains to the way that we can figure out how to like, appreciate, and acknowledge new and distinctive things. We can figure out how to be better grateful audience.

3.   *Informative Listening*

Informative listening is the name we provide for the situation where the audience's essential concern is to understand the message. Audience members are assumed to be satisfied if seeing that the importance they appoint to messages is as close as could be allowed to that which the sender expected.

Instructive tuning in, or listening to comprehend, is found in all parts of our lives. A lot of our learning comes from this type of listening. Case in point, we listen to lectures or guidelines from instructors—and what we learn relies upon how well we tune in. In the work environment, we tune in to see new practices or systems—and how well we perform also relies upon how well we tune in. We listen to guidelines, briefings, reports, and talks; on the off chance that we tune in ineffectively, we aren't furnished with the data we require.

Now and again, being careful on informative listening is quite challenging. Whatever the case, powerful informative listening requests that you focus unequivocally on the message—and know its source.

There are three key variables identified with useful informative listening. Knowing these variables can help you start to enhance your informative listening abilities; that is, you will turn out to be progressively effective in comprehension what the speaker implies.

1. *Vocabulary*. The exact relationship between vocabulary and listening has never been resolved; however it is clear that expanding your vocabulary will build your potential for better comprehension. What's more, it's never past the point of no return to enhance your vocabulary. Having a veritable enthusiasm for words and dialect, trying to learn new words, separating new words into their segment parts—every one of these things will help you move forward to your vocabulary.

Another great approach to enhance your vocabulary is to be touchy to the connection in which words are utilized. Sometimes, new words show up with equivalent words.

Incidentally, a new word is utilized to outline a circumstance or quality. Search for these and other logical intimations to help you learn new words and enhance your vocabulary.

2. *Focus*. Focus is quite troublesome. You can recall times when someone else was not concentrating on what you were stating—and you likely can recall times when you were not focusing on something that somebody was stating to you.

There are numerous reasons individuals don't think when tuning in. Now and again audience members attempt to isolate their consideration between two contending stimuli. At different times, audience members are distracted with an option that is other than the speaker of the occasion. Some of the time audience members are excessively personal, or excessively concerned with their own particular needs, making it impossible to focus on the message being conveyed. On the other hand maybe they need interest vitality, or hobby. Numerous individuals essentially have not learned to think while tuning in. Others simply decline to discipline themselves, without the inspiration to acknowledge responsibility for good tuning in. Fixation obliges discipline, inspiration, and acknowledgment of obligation.

3. *Memory*. Memory is a particularly essential variable to enlightening tuning in; you can't handle data without bringing

memory into play. All the more particularly, memory helps your useful informative listening in three beneficial ways.

a. It permits you to review encounters and data important to capacity in your general surroundings. In other words, without memory you would have no information bank.

b. It sets up desires concerning what you will experience. You would be not able to drive in substantial activity, respond to new circumstances, or settle on basic choices in life without memory of your past encounters.

c. It permits you to comprehend what others say. Without basic memory of the significance of words, you could not correspond with any other person. Without memory of ideas and thoughts, you couldn't comprehend the meaning

4.   ***Relationship Listening***

The reason for relationship listening is either to help an individual or to enhance the relationship between individuals.

Remedial listening is an uncommon sort of relationship listening. Remedial listening infers circumstances where advocates, therapeutic work force, or different experts permit a harried individual to talk through an issue. Be that as it may it can likewise be utilized when you listen to companions or colleagues and permit them to "breathe out and help them get heavy things off of their chests."

Despite the fact that relationship listening obliges you to listen for data, the accentuation is on comprehending or understanding the other individual. Three practices are critical to compelling relationship tuning in: paying attention, showing of support, and understanding.

1. *Paying Attention*. Much has been said in regards to the significance of "focusing," or "paying attention" conduct. In relationship type of listening, "paying attention" practices show that the audience is concentrating on the speaker. Nonverbal signals are pivotal in relationship tuning in; that is, your nonverbal conduct shows that you are taking care of the speaker— otherwise that you aren't.

Eye contact is a standout amongst the most vital "paying attention" practices. Looking fittingly and easily at the speaker communicates something specific that is not quite the same as that sent by a successive movement of look, gazing, or checking out the room. Body situating imparts acknowledgment or need of it. Inclining forward, around the speaker, illustrates enthusiasm; inclining ceaselessly imparts absence of hobby. Head gestures, grins, glares, and vocalized signs, for example, "I see," "uh-huh" or "yes"— all are sure "paying attention" practices. A charming manner of speaking, tender touching, and sympathy toward the other individual's solace are other "paying attention" practices.

2. *Showing of Support*. Numerous reactions have a negative or non - strong impact; for instance, intruding on the speaker, changing the subject, turning the discussion toward you, and showing an absence of sympathy toward the other individual. Giving guidance, endeavoring to control the discussion, or demonstrating that you see yourself as predominant are different practices that will have an unfriendly impact on the relationship.

In some cases the best reaction is hush. The speaker may require a "sounding board," not a "resonating board." Insightful relationship audience members know when to talk and when to simply listen—and they by and large listen more than they talk. Three qualities portray steady audience members: (1) watchfulness—being cautious about what they say and do; (2) conviction—communicating trust in the capacity of the other individual; and (3) tolerance—being willing to give others the time they have to communicate sufficiently.

3. *Understanding*. What is compassion or empathy? Do not confuse it with sympathy, which is an inclination for or about another. It doesn't also confound with apathy which is lack of

care; an absence of feeling. Compassion or Empathy is feeling and considering things *with* someone else. The minding, empathic audience is capable to go into the universe of another—to see as alternate sees, hear as alternate listens, and feel as alternate feels. Clearly, the individual who has had more experience and lived longer stands a superior shot of being a successful empathic audience. The individual who has never been separated, lost a son to death, been bankrupt, or lost work may have a more troublesome time identifying with individuals with these issues than one who has encountered such things.

With all these things being said, we could somehow conclude that risk is included with being an empathic relationship audience. You can't be a compelling empathic audience without getting to be included, which now and again implies adapting more than you truly need to know. Be that as it may, authorities can't charge viably, supervisors can't regulate skillfully, and people can't relate interpersonally without compassion. Abraham Lincoln is accounted for to have said, "I feel frustrated about the man who can't feel the stripes upon the back of another." Truly, the individuals who can't feel with someone else are off guard in comprehending that individual. Empathic conduct can be found out. To begin with, you should learn as much as you can about the other individual. Second, you must acknowledge the other individual—regardless of the fact that

you can't acknowledge a few parts of that individual's conduct. Third, you must have the craving to be an empathic audience. What's more, you must recollect that compassion is urgent to viable relationship listening.

5. *Bias Listening*

The last kind of listening (though there may be a lot more we cannot all discuss) is Bias Listening. It may be the most imperative sort, for it is fundamental to the next four. By being delicate to changes in the speaker's rate, volume, drive, pitch, and accentuation, the enlightening audience can identify even subtleties of distinction in significance. By detecting the effect of specific reactions, for example, "uh huh," or "I see," relationship listening can be reinforced. Location of contrasts between sounds made by certain instruments in the ensemble, or parts sung by the a cappella vocal gathering, improves appreciative tuning in. At long last, affectability to delays, and other vocal and nonverbal signals, permits basic audience members to all the more precisely judge the speaker's message, as well as his expectations too.

Clearly, numerous individuals have great bias listening capacity in a few territories however not in others. With all these being said, even though this bias type of listening cuts over the other four sorts of tuning in, there are three things to consider about this kind.

1. *Capacity to Hear Well*. Clearly, individuals who do not have the capacity to hear well will have more noteworthy trouble in segregating among sounds. Regularly this issue is more intense for a few frequencies, or pitches, than others. Case in point, an individual may be less ready to separate thoughts, ideas or signals when the sound is originating from a bass voice than from a higher pitched one.

2. *Consciousness of sound structure.* Local speakers get to be very capable at perceiving vowel and consonant sounds that do or don't show up toward the starting, middle, or end of words. Regard for the sound structure of the dialect will lead to more capable oppressive tuning in. A man who pays consideration on sound structure would perceive that a quickly spoken "Idrankitfirst" could mean it is possible that "I drank it first" or "I'd rank it first." Recognition of the two implications would bring about the audience to look for clarification.

3. *Mix of nonverbal signs*. The past section pointed out how activity, non-action, and vocal variables were essential in comprehension messages. No place is consideration regarding these figures more essential than compelling discriminative tuning in. Words don't generally convey genuine emotions. The

way they are said, or the way the speaker acts, may be the way to understanding the genuine or expected significance.

Compelling tuning in, whether useful, social, thankful, basic, or discriminative, obliges ability. In a few cases, the aptitudes are the same for the different sorts of tuning in; now and again, they are truly distinctive. The next part will give you rules for better tuning in. It will likewise let you know which aptitudes are particularly discriminating for every kind of tuning in.

Step by step instructions to be an Effective Listener

This section is a prescriptive one. It offers pragmatic proposals on the most proficient method to be a superior audience.

While there are numerous approaches to build a rundown of proposals, we will consider them as far as what works best in three noteworthy classifications:

1. What you think about tuning in.

2. What you feel about tuning in.

3. What you do about tuning in.

You can figure out how to listen viably; take a gander at the segments of that learning: considering, feeling, doing.

What You Think about Listening

Even though considering, feeling, and doing go as one, the reasoning (or psychological) space of learning is maybe the best place to start. All things considered, successful listening takes exertion—it obliges most extreme intuition power. Here are six proposals.

1. *Comprehend the complexities of tuning in*. The majority of us underestimate great tuning in. In this manner, we don't work hard at making strides. Be that as it may, listening is a perplexing action, what's more, its multifaceted nature clarifies the accentuation given in past parts to understanding the deceptions, forms, also, sorts of tuning in. Knowing the errors about listening can keep you from being caught by them. Realizing that the procedure includes more than simply accepting messages will help you concentrate on receiving as well as alternate segments too. Perceiving the five noteworthy sorts of listening will help you to intentionally immediate your energies toward the sort of listening needed for the condition existing apart from everything else. Listening requires a dynamic reaction, not a latent one. Compelling listening doesn't simply happen; it takes thought—and intuition can be diligent work. In any case, there is no other approach to turn into a compelling audience. Consider the complexities of tuning in, and work to comprehend them.

2. *Get ready to Listen*. Readiness comprises of three stages— long haul, mid-term, and short-term. We said prior that turning into a viable audience is a lifetime try; at the end of the day, growing your listening capacity will be a continuous errand. Be that as it may, there are two things you can do to enhance your listening abilities for the long haul: (a) work on listening to troublesome material and (b) construct your vocabulary. A lot of individuals essentially don't challenge their tuning in capacity. Since the greater part of today's radio and TV projects don't oblige concentrated or watchful tuning in, your listening abilities don't enhance through proceeded introduction to them. Also, you need to extend on the off chance that you need to develop. Compel yourself to listen deliberately to congressional verbal confrontations, addresses, sermons, or other material that requires focus. Building your vocabulary will enhance your conversational abilities and you're perusing aptitudes and in addition your listening abilities. Furthermore, the more words you take in, the better audience you will get to be.

Mid-term readiness for listening obliges that you do the vital foundation study before the listening starts. Foundation papers, pre-briefs, and a development look at a printed version (or an electronic presentation) of instructions slides on the other hand outlines will help you in being prepared to tune in.

Transient arrangement may be characterized as a prompt status to tune in. At the point when the speaker's mouth opens, you ought to open your ears. That is not the time to be chasing for a pen, checking a letter from home, or considering about some random subject. Great audience members—better than average audience members—are in the "spring-stacked position to tune in." It is essential to get ready to listen.

3. *Change in accordance with the circumstance*. No listening circumstance is precisely the same as another. The time, the speaker, the message—all change. Be that as it may, numerous different variables additionally influence tuning in, however less clearly so: physiological variables for example, rest, craving, solace, perseverance; mental variables, for example, passionate strength, affinity with the speaker, information of the subject; and physical components for example, size and shading of the room. Clearly, some of these things will have a constructive outcome on your tuning in while others will have a negative impact. A thick remote accent, poor language structure, a room with poor acoustics, and the subject of the past speaker—all may exhibit uncommon obstructions to viable tuning in. Be that as it may, being mindful of the obstructions and pondering how to overcome them can help you enhance the circumstance.

Great audience members are never caught into suspecting that any correspondence exchange or listening circumstance is precisely like whatever other. The Grecian scholar Heraclitus said it well: "You can't venture into the same stream twice." Things change. By considering the special components of the circumstance, you can do your best work as an audience. Change in accordance with the circumstance.

4. *Concentrate on thoughts or key focuses*. On occasion, you may get it the procedure, you may have arranged well, and you may have the capacity to change in accordance with the circumstance—yet you come up short as an audience. This disappointment results on the grounds that you didn't listen to the right things. For instance, you may recollect an interesting story the speaker advised to make a point; however you overlooked what's really important. Others gloat, "I listen just for the actualities." By focusing only on individual supporting truths, they might really miss the fundamental thoughts. Actualities A, B, and C may be fascinating in their own particular right, however the speaker's explanation behind offering them is more often than not to add to a speculation from them. Speculations, not certainties, are typically generally critical. In studies directed a few years prior at the University of New Mexico, it was found out that understudies who did best on everything except taking repetition memory examinations were the individuals who tuned in for key focuses and thoughts. Interestingly, the individuals who endeavored to remember

moment points of interest improved on low-level repetition memory exams than the people who concentrated on thoughts— and they did much more awful when long haul maintenance was the paradigm. While there are a few special cases, as when listening for headings to somebody's home or remembering a scientific equation, it is generally best to concentrate on thoughts or key focuses.

5. *Exploit the rate differential.* Thought can work much quicker than discourse. A normal individual may talk a few words a second—120 to 180 words a minute. In blasts of excitement, we may even talk a minimal quicker. Most open speakers talk to some degree slower, particularly to expansive groups of onlookers. Yet most audience member can process up to 500 words for each moment, contingent upon the nature and trouble of the material. Pressure is proficient through methodical evacuation of little sections—so little that contortion is not able to see by audience members. Tests in which listening time is sliced down the middle—an hour address is listened to in a fraction of the time—uncover little, if any, critical misfortune in listening and learning. In fact, audience members are prepared for a break in light of the fact that there is no time for their psyches to meander. Viable listening obliges hard considering, particularly if the material is testing. The aftereffects of these tests point to the likelihood of profiting by the velocity

differential. Tragically, the difference between pace of thought and rate of discourse may indicate that a person is unconsciously daydreaming or focusing on something other than what is being said. This is not the situation with great audience members, on the other hand; they utilize the time differential to great favorable position. They compress, expect, and detail inquiries in light of the speaker's message.

6. *Sort out material for learning*. Clearly, speakers can improve listening through watchful association and presentation of thoughts. What's more, if inquiries are suitable, you can look for elucidation of any focuses you neglect to get. Frequently, be that as it may, addressing is not allowed or, maybe because of time requirements or the span of the audience is unseemly. What would you be able to do? Recalling that the pace differential exists; you can orchestrate the material in your psyche or in your notes as its being introduced. This will help you comprehend and recollect that it later. You can set yourself up to hold the data to be exhibited by posing these questions:

What point is the speaker attempting to make? What principle thoughts would it be a good idea for me to recollect? How does this data re late to what I definitely know? Rearranging the material you have to learn, and looking for connections between the new material and what you definitely know, obliges concentrated considering. It is less demanding to just "block out."

What You Feel about Listening

We started by examining what you think about tuning in since powerful listening requires thorough psychological preparing, or thought. Be that as it may, ownership of the most honed psyche won't make you a decent audience if your sentiments are off base. At the end of the day, what you feel about listening is imperative. Here are six proposals for enhancing your "feel" for tuning in.

1. *Need to tune in*. This proposal is fundamental to all others, for it just says that you must have an expectation to tune in. We can sum up the total of what review of having been compelled to listen to a discourse or a preparation that we would not generally like to listen to. What's more, tuning in under coercion from time to time results in comprehension or happiness, despite the fact that there are special cases. Maybe you have attended a meeting or a get-together out of a feeling of obligation, yet discovered it to have been beneficial. What may be the reason? Likely, since you arrived, you chose to make the best of the circumstance; that is, you decided to tune in.

In some cases you would prefer not to tune in. At different times, your activities may demonstrate that you would prefer not to tune in when you truly do. At still different times, you may be uninformed that you would prefer not to tune in. Every one of the three of circumstances is full of feeling or attitudinal; that is, they include your sentiments about tuning in.

2. *Delay judgment*. There are times when you must be a basic or judgmental audience. You must measure the benefits of what the speaker is stating. Now and again, you must make critical choices taking into account what you listen. There are additionally times when you must judge the speaker. Prospective employee meet-ups, battle guarantees, discourse challenges—all are samples of where judgment of the speaker is vital. The issue is, however, that you may be judgmental when you shouldn't be. You may judge the speaker rather than the substance, or you may shape judgments before the speaker has wrapped up.

A kid who was one month short of being 16 chosen to admit to his dad that he had driven the family auto on the earlier night. His more youthful sister's guaranteed ride to acrobatic class hadn't arrived, and it was the night of her last practice before an execution. So he made the choice to take her despite the fact that he didn't yet have a driver's permit. He was additionally certain that he hadn't been seen and would never be figured out. Still, his still, small voice was irritating him and his family had pushed genuineness and openness. He chose to tell his dad.

After listening to that the kid had taken the auto, his dad got to be angry. He hardly heard the reason, and he neglected to consider that the kid had taken it upon himself to admit. He told the kid that the demonstration would postpone his getting a driver's permit by two months. At that point the father reconsidered the circumstance and said, "Child, I acted quickly. My feelings outwitted me. You were wrong to drive the auto on the grounds that you infringed upon the law. Be that as it may, to be honest, I am glad for you for three reasons: you got your sister to tumbling practice, you spoke the truth about it, and most importantly, you are my child."

Managers frequently ask why individuals in their association won't level with them. They require just considering the messenger in old Rome who paid with his life for bringing awful news. An old Turkish maxim says, "Messenger with awful news ought to keep one foot in the stirrup." Delaying judgment and judging the substance as opposed to the speaker will prompt better listening and more legit correspondence.

3. *Concede your inclinations*. Let's be honest: Everyone is human! We all have likes and abhorrence; a few things turn us on, others turn us off. These qualities are characteristic and not out of the ordinary. The issue comes when we let our predispositions—our preferences and aversions—impede understanding the speaker's message.

For instance, assume you have had three terrible encounters with individuals from a certain place and you discover that the speaker you now hear is from that exact place. You might tend to instantly doubt him, or to ruin whatever he needs to say. Just by conceding your preference against individuals from that place will you have the capacity to think past your past experience and listen adequately to what this speaker needs to say? Before you dismiss the above case as unessential, consider a period in your past when you got suddenly sick after eating a certain snack. You knew the disorder was brought about by an infection and not the snack, but rather it was a long time before that snack again tasted great to you. In a comparative manner, predisposition from past experience can impact what you hear and the importance you get from it. In the event that you need to be a powerful audience, you must know and concede your inclinations.

4. *Try not to block out "dry" subjects*. At whatever point you are enticed to "block out" something in light of the fact that you think it will be exhausting or futile, recall that you can't assess the significance of the message until you have heard it. By then, it is most likely past the point where it is possible to request that the speaker rehash everything that was said; the chance to listen adequately will have passed. As was expressed before, you should mean to tune in.

Listed in here are several suggestions to keep your concentration or focus when the subject appears to be dry.

a. Place yourself in the speaker's place. Attempt to see the speaker's perspective, and attempt to comprehend the speaker's disposition toward the subject.

b. Regularly review what the speaker has said. Attempt to condense the message as the speaker would compress it.

c. Continually get some information about what the speaker is stating: How would I be able to utilize this data? In what manner would I be able to impart this data to others? What else could be said in regards to this subject?

d. Ask yourself, "What does the speaker realize that I don't?"

e. Find no less than one noteworthy application or conclusion from each message you listen. At the end of the day, ask "what's in this message for me?" Then discover the answer.

f. Listen just as you will be obliged to show the same message to an alternate gathering of people later.

Compelling audience members have found the benefit of listening to messages they may have at first thought to be "dry." Once in a while the messages aren't so dry all things considered. Also, even when they are, there still may be something of quality in them.

5. *Acknowledge obligation regarding comprehension*. Try not to expect this disposition: "Here I am! Show me—in the event that you can." Such audience members trust information can be filled them as water is filled a container. Also, they trust the obligation rests with the one doing the pouring; that is, they trust it is the speaker's flaw if powerful listening does not happen.

A speaker bears an extensive obligation regarding how well the gathering of people tunes in. Also, the speaker's unmistakable association, connecting with support materials, and proper conveyance do indeed guide tuning in. In any case, great audience members are great on the grounds that they acknowledge the obligation regarding listening and comprehension.

6. *Urge others to talk*. This point applies to those circumstances in which you discover yourself "one-on-one," in a little gathering talk, or some other setting that requires trades of vocal correspondence. However, you can't listen if nobody is talking. The initial two rules of this segment (conveying that you need to listen and being willing to postpone judgment) are wellsprings of support to speakers. The talk underneath spreads a few other things you can do.

a. Quit talking. You can't listen in case you're talking.

b. Give positive input. Look and act intrigued. Positive head gestures, sharpness, and grins—all offer consolation to the speaker.

c. Make inquiries. Questions that show interest and consideration support both speaker and audience. Demonstrate your interest.

d. Relate to the speaker. Placed yourself in the speaker's place; this will help you comprehend the message.

e. Keep up the confidence. On the off chance that the data is touchy, try not to impart it to others.

f. Offer ideas or information. We have a tendency to advise things to those who let us know things. So in the event that you need the speaker to share ideas with you, impart it to the speaker.

What You Do about Listening

What we think about listening and what we feel about listening are both essential to capable tuning in. In any case the aptitudes themselves are urgent. Aptitudes frame the psychomotor— the "doing"— component of tuning in. Here are six pivotal aptitudes.

1. Set up eye contact with the speaker. Studies show that listening has a positive association with eye contact.

As such, the better eye contact with you with the speaker, the better you will tune in. Keeping in mind the use of eye contact is particularly vital in relationship tuning in, it is too vital for alternate sorts of tuning in: informative, appreciative, analytical, bias.

There are a few things you can do to set up positive eye contact with the speaker:

a. In one-on-one or little gathering settings, sit or stand where you can take a gander at the individual doing the talking.

b. In expansive or big gatherings, sit up front of the gathering of people. You can all the more effectively build up eye contact with the speaker from this vantage point.

c. Try not to get so included in taking notes that you neglect to take a gander at the speaker. The speaker's motions, movements, and outward appearance are frequently an essential part of the message.

d. Oppose the enticement to let something about the room, or items inside and around the room, divert you. Concentrate on the speaker and the message.

e. Try not to take a gander at other people who enter or leave while the speaker is talking. This practice not just intrudes on your line of reasoning—it adds to the diversion of the speaker.

f. Speakers now and then display a visual guide too early, or disregard to evacuate it when they have completed the process of utilizing it. Concentrate on the visual guide just when it is a resource for the point being examined.

A last point merits discourse: Never rest when somebody is conversing with you. This point may appear self-evident. Yet, let's be honest—in the "hastiness" of our lives, we have a tendency to end up uninvolved at whatever point we tune in. Detachment advances lessened consideration, which thus permits drowsiness to happen. By and large, it is ideal to stand up or indeed, even to leave the room, as opposed to nod off.

2. *Take notes viably*. A few individuals suggest that you not take notes so you can focus your consideration completely on what the speaker is stating. This practice functions admirably for audience members who are honored with an awesome memory; the majority of us aren't. Taking notes won't just help you recall that, it will help you compose what the speaker is stating. What's more, it may even guide your understanding and maintenance— all things considered; compelling note taking will oblige you to think.

There are a wide range of approaches to take notes; for example, straight lying out, mind mapping, and pivotal word strategy. Ask distinctive individuals what technique they utilize, and then discover what works best for you. Whatever technique you select then again devise, a few things merit considering.

a. Try not to endeavor to record everything. As specified prior, compelling audience members concentrate on the key thoughts or primary focuses.

b. Compose plainly enough that you can comprehend your composing later. If not, make sure that you permit time to interpret your notes before they develop feeling dead or cold. It's crippling to audit your notes two weeks after the fact just to discover that they have neither rhyme nor reason.

c. Try not to depend on listening later to a tape of the discourse. Think. Will you have room schedule-wise? Taking a gander at your notes for five minutes is by and large adequate, and is a great deal more time-productive than listening to the whole discourse once more.

d. Circle or highlight the most imperative focuses.

3. *Be a physically included audience*. Exactly what does this proclamation mean? As you have as of now seen, listening requires more than simply hearing. You have likewise seen that looking and taking notes will help to keep you from getting to be inactive. Be that as it may, there is more: Active tuning in takes

vitality and association. Here are some physical practices that will guarantee your association and help you're tuning in.

a. Utilize great stance. Sit up straight, yet easily. Great stance helps breathing and readiness. It additionally conveys positive enthusiasm to the speaker.

b. Take after the speaker. On the off chance that the speaker moves, turn your head or turn in your seat to keep up eye contact and consideration. This development additionally helps in keeping you caution.

c. Try not to be an empty. Outward appearances, head gestures, also, tilts of the head demonstrate your contribution and give positive input to the speaker.

d. Utilize your hands to take notes, as well as to show regard by acclaim when proper.

e. Take part when crowd inclusion is empowered. Make inquiries. React when a show of hands is called for. Be a dynamic audience.

f. Wear a smile.

4. Maintain a strategic distance from negative characteristics. Everybody has idiosyncrasies.

Watch anybody for a stretch of time and you will be persuaded of this. On the off chance that your characteristics don't bring about a negative response, don't stress over them. On the off chance that a characteristic is certain or empowering and brings a positive reaction, give careful consideration to do it all the more regularly. Lamentably, a few characteristics are negative or diverting. These should be maintained a strategic distance from.

Here are a few samples of audience characteristics that either thwart listening or have a negative effect—on the speaker or on different audience members. Keep away from these peculiarities.

a. Squirming, tapping a pencil, or playing with an elastic band or some other article. The impact on you may be impartial; however such things divert different audience members and are an inconvenience to the speaker.

b. Ceaselessly taking a gander at the clock or your watch.

c. Checking a paper, adjusting a check book, organizing things in your wallet, or participating in other conduct which detracts focus from the speaker and message. To put it plainly, any peculiarity or conduct that takes away from the speaker or the message ought to be dodged. Such things impede the speaker, occupy the consideration of different audience members, what's more, keep you from being the best audience you can be.

5. Exercise your listening muscles. Really, there are no muscles actually included with listening—however this thought advises us that listening takes hone. Generally as a competitor must work out consistently and a performer must practice every day, so you must work reliably to be a viable audience.

Be that as it may, reliable practice in itself is insufficient. The trouble of the message is additionally essential. Presentation to testing material and troublesome listening circumstances will extend your capacity and construct you're listening muscles. Cases in point, let us assume you realized that you would be obliged to convey a 50-pound weight one hundred yards in under a moment. You wouldn't rehearse via conveying a 30-pound weight. You would rehearse via conveying no less than a 50-pound weight, and you most likely would condition yourself to convey it more than 100 yards in under a moment. With this sort of practice, you would be more than equivalent to the errand. Thus it is with tuning in: Practice to at any rate the level you will be obliged to perform—maybe a touch above. At long last, "s-t-r-e-t-c-h" your vocabulary. We've said this sometime recently, however nothing will pay more noteworthy listening profits. Take in the implications of new words and acronyms. Listen to and read learning materials that contain testing words. Keep a word reference close-by. Gaze upward new words as you read them; on the other hand scribble them down as you listen so you can gaze upward the implications later.

6. Take after the Golden Rule. Do unto others as you would have them do unto you. The center of all powerful correspondence is "different directedness." There are exemptions to most other listening principles. For instance, there are times when an audience shouldn't plan; readiness might forestall openness to new thoughts. There are times when the target is not to concentrate on key focuses, but rather to listen for subordinate thoughts or supporting material. There are times when we ought not to defer judgment—yet we must act. In any case while these and different guidelines have exemptions, not so for the Golden Rule. The viable audience is constantly other coordinated, concentrated on the other individual.

Be the sort of audience you need others to be the point at which you are talking. Ask, "How might I need others to listen to me?" That's the manner by which to be a compelling listener or audience.

Common Misconceptions of Listening

False notion #1: Smarter Individuals Are Better Listeners

Clearly, knowledge assumes a part in a man's capacity to tune in. Persons with constrained insight will be limited in their ability to transform the data contained in messages they get. Then again, those having high insight levels will have a more noteworthy preparing capacity. Yet, the conviction that "more intelligent individuals are better listeners" is frequently false. Truth be told, some studies recommends that the reverse is frequently genuine.

It's because being smart isn't just about being able to listen better. It can also be genetic. Some people simply have superhuman abilities to hear something once – even without paying active attention – and immediately remember or understand it. Also, being too smart can actually result in very poor social skills, among which is listening. It's because many smart people feel they already know everything, which renders listening a meaningless exercise.

The act of listening while it is true that it needed mind skills often than not require emotional skills too like the act of listening intently and paying attention to the speaker; with that in mind we cannot clearly say that more intelligent people have the capacity to listen well than those who are below their mind skills level. In fact, many people who don't consider themselves smart pay more attention and listen better because they know they need to in order to compensate for their lack of aptitude. Using that logic alone, it's already a foregone conclusion that smarter people aren't necessarily good listeners.

False notion #2: Avid Readers Are Better Listeners

This particular notion is often untrue, despite the fact that both act of reading and listening rely on the interpretation of words into meaning. On account of the mutual interpretation capacity, there is clearly some sort of relationship in the middle of both; the issue is numerous individuals erroneously accept that every single great reader is essentially a great audience member.

It's actually possible that avid readers may not care so much to listen to others on the basis that since they read a lot, they know a lot – probably more than most people. As with being so smart, some avid readers may think why else do I need to listen to other people when I am already and continue to grow smarter by doing what I love to do, which is reading. Again, it's not necessarily the case that avid readers are automatically good listeners. Some are, some aren't.

Specialists who direct diverse standard reading tests to the same individual locate a high positive correlation between the two arrangements of scores; that is, persons who score well on one reading test for the most part score well on another while persons who score low on one test tend to score low on another. Specialists who test individuals on institutionalized listening tests find comparable results. The individuals who score high on one test have a tendency to score high on another and bad habit versa. Interestingly, then again, there is frequently a shockingly low connection between one's scores on reading tests and that same individual's scores on listening tests. For a more detailed example of this outcome, consider the accompanying test.

An instructor separates a class into two segments, arbitrarily doling out novices until every segment has a large portion of them. Each new "class" is put in another, separate classroom. Everyone in class is given a short paper, advised to read it once and after that place it on the work area, clear side up. Novices in alternate class listen as the educator conveys the paper as a discourse. All novices in both classes are then given indistinguishable tests on the material secured. Analyses like this one reliably bring about certain inquiries being addressed effectively all the more frequently by those who read the paper while different inquiries are replied effectively all the more regularly by the individuals who heard it conveyed as a discourse. This outcome is truly not too astounding. At the point when we read a report, visual signs—edges, delineations, and accentuation—get to be elements. Then again, when we tune in, the speaker's vocal accentuation, perusing style, delays, and so forth impact our comprehension. There is, then, a contrast between handling data from the composed word and handling it from the talked word. The way that a few individuals are preferable at one over the other shows the misrepresentation of trusting that great readers are fundamentally great audience members. By the way, test outcomes likewise demonstrate that great many people score higher as readers than as audience members. Being a person who is good in reading doesn't ensure that the same person is a good listener as well.

False notion #3: Listening Is Not My Problem

Some individuals usually think they are better listeners than many others. It is the individuals they work for, the ones who work with or for them, their relatives, furthermore, their companions who have an issue in listening effectively—not themselves.

As it is normally thought of, it is easy to pinpoint other person's mistakes than to admit ours. Sometimes the real problem is within us but we don't have the courage to admit so.

Pride is the number one reason for this. For many people, it's inconceivable that they don't know how to do something as "simple" as listening. "What a travesty to my personhood!" some might exclaim. But as you now know, listening isn't a simple activity. It actually takes a certain skill and self-control level to be able to listen to other people well.

Another reason for this belief is today's prevailing culture, especially among the youth. We are living in what many sociology experts coined as the "selfie generation", named after the tendency to take pictures of selves. The selfie phenomenon is adjudged as a narcissistic behavior, i.e., self-centeredness, and listening requires paying less or no attention to one's self in order to focus on the other person. As such, many people feel that listening is not their problem because their priority is, consistent with living in the selfie generation, themselves.

Another reason for this mentality when it comes to listening is that the perception that poor listening skills isn't a problem to begin with. Why would people think it's their problem when it's not supposed to be one in the first place? Which leads to the last reason for thinking this way: ignorance.

People won't recognize a problem to be such if they don't know it is. Let's be honest, nobody ever died, went bankrupt or acquired a deadly disease on account of being a poor listener, right? In that regard, people don't see poor listening skills as a problem per se. If they don't see it's a problem to begin with, the more they won't acknowledge that it's their problem.

As communication is a two-way process, we ought to take responsibility to listen well. The act of listening takes a bit of effort for communication to become effective.

False notion #4: Listening and Hearing Are the Same

Just having great hearing does not make one a decent audience. Truth be told, numerous individuals who have flawlessly great hearing are bad audience members. Having great hearing does encourage one's view of sound; however great audience members don't just hear words—they concentrate on the importance. We correspond adequately with one another seeing that we offer importance.

In the event that I let you know something and you misjudge me, successful correspondence has not happened. On the off chance that I let you know something and you comprehend what I implied—that is, if we have a successful exchange or sharing of significance—we say that the correspondence is successful. Successful tuning in infers that the audience comprehends what the speaker implies.

The contrast in the middle of hearing and listening can be expressed along these lines: Hearing is the gathering of sound, listening is the connection of intending to the sound. Hearing is detached, listening is dynamic. Understanding the distinction in the middle of listening to and listening is an essential for listening success.

I remember one instance where a friend rebuked me. She was telling me about a particular problem she was encountering at that time and the steps she was taking to address it. I knew I heard everything she said because we were in a quiet place and I wasn't distracted by anything in that place. When the time came that she was asking what next steps she should take to address the problem better, the advice I gave turned out to be something she had already done, which she already divulged early in the conversation. She said she felt bad that I wasn't listening. I told her I heard everything she said, which she acknowledged to be true. She said that if I also listened to what I was hearing from her, I would've given a different advice. I merely gathered sound and didn't connect with her intentions.

Many times, people say, "I hear ya!" I think it should be changed to "I'm listening to ya!" It would make the world a better place.

The last way that hearing and listening are different is in action. If I say, "please give me a glass of water." and you got me a glass of water, you were listening. If all you did was say "Alright!" but you never acted on it, you just heard me and my sound. Hearing is passive, listening is active.

False Notion #5: Age comes along with Listening Skills

Unquestionably, the limit or capacity to listen and add essential meanings to messages enhances with age and experience—in the early years and at any rate to some point. Yet, even though the listening capacity progresses, its execution may basically decline at some area. In any case this doesn't need to be the situation. The disparity between listening capacity and listening execution is regularly because of us having adapted awful listening propensities. Here are some of the most widely recognized unfortunate propensities.

1. Adapting not to tune in. We take in a considerable measure about not listening while growing up. Case in point, a guardian lets us know: "Bear in mind to wear your jacket to class!" But we don't need to wear one, so we "learn" to not tune in. Later, at school, the educator rehashes a task a few times, planning to make sure that every one of the students has heard it. The instructor's conduct strengthens not to tune in, since there will be various open doors for us to get the information. Another case is found in the idea given to repetition in radio and TV publicizing. This reiteration further conditions us against listening painstakingly the first time.

2. Contemplating what we are going to say as opposed to listening to the speaker. In attempting to arrange our reaction, we frequently overlook what's really important that the other individual is making. At that point, when we do talk, it seems as though we weren't listening— which is precisely what happened.

3. Talking when we ought to be tuning in. Our whole culture appears to condition us to talk, not to tune in. The quiet demonstration of listening appears to be no match for the messages heaved at us ceaselessly. The best approaches to control things—to have things go our path—seem to be by all accounts by out-talking others. Some legitimize this conduct by saying, "the squeaky wheel gets the oil." But the reality of the situation is that we miss a ton by talking when we ought to be tuning in. A savvy individual once thought that we ought to spend twice as much time listening as talking since we were made with one mouth and two ears. A greater amount of us ought to regard this counsel.

4. Listening to what we hope to hear as opposed to what is really said. This propensity appears to turn into an undeniably more prominent issue as we develop more seasoned. Listening to what we expect as opposed to what the other individual means can represent a major issue. Whether we are listening to learn, assess, segregate, unwind, or enhance a relationship, it's vital to listen to the next individual.

5. Not focusing. The name of this unfortunate propensity says it all. There are some other basic variables that cause us to not focus.

Distraction: Infrequently we don't listen in light of the fact that we are engrossed. We have such a variety of things to consider. Our psyche is brimming with thoughts, certainties, and stresses. We are not able to set them aside while we tune in. By and by, great listening requests that we maintain a strategic distance from distraction when somebody is identifying with us.

Bias: States of mind and sentiments not tempered by logical intuition can prompt partiality. Maybe we don't care for the speaker. On the other hand the subject may be one that we know little about and "would prefer not to know." Maybe we don't care for the strategy for presentation. In any occasion, we are biased against the presentation; we have prejudged it. Consequently, we might rationally contend with the speaker. Alternately we may basically "block out." Prejudicial intuition can redirect our consideration far from what the speaker is stating.

Egotism: Since we live with ourselves throughout the day consistently, the greater part of us invests considerably more energy contemplating ourselves than about others. It is in this way not surprising that self-concern meddles with our listening to what another is stating. We must work at exchanging our focus from "I" to "You"— from ourselves to the individual doing the talking.

Stereotyping: As individuals, we hold certain convictions around a mixed bag of subjects. We have "settled" judgments or ideas that we accept to be genuine and right. On the off chance that a speaker facts that contradict our convictions, we have a tendency to disregard what is being said—either on the grounds that it is not acceptable to us or in light of the fact that we don't need our thoughts tested. Great audience members don't permit themselves to be caught by stereotypes.

False notion #6: Listening Skills Are Difficult to Learn

Really, the aptitudes themselves are not all that difficult—and introductory advancement is fast. Be that as it may, figuring out how to apply the aptitudes reliably does take diligent work. Furthermore, getting to be truly capable takes much time and practice—a lifetime to be correct. In any case, the exertion is without a doubt beneficial. We have to comprehend the procedure of listening and the sorts of tuning in.

In most cases, whether it's choosing to listen, learning to listen or other things, attitude determines the altitude.   In other words, the way people look at something often sets the tone as to how much success they can experience in it.   If I already decided in my mind that learning how to listen well is hard, then my subconscious mind will enact that belief and will cause my mind to have a difficult time learning how to listen well, even if doing so doesn't really require the I.Q. of a genius. Often times a person's "I will" is more important than his or her "I can."

When we look at people like Thomas Edison who suffered so many failed attempts at the light bulb before finally getting it right, we are reminded of the power of attitude in succeeding in things we set out to accomplish. If his attitude was it's going to be too hard to create the light bulb, if not impossible, he couldn't have persisted through the numerous failed experiments and achieved success. But because he didn't think of it that way, he succeeded.

When we learn to accept the fact that listening skills aren't rocket science, half the battle is already won.

The Process of Listening

We said before that the initial phase in listening successfully is to perceive certain errors or false ideas. The following step is to comprehend the procedure.

Listening is an intricate procedure—an essential piece of the all-out correspondence process, though a section frequently overlooked. This disregard comes about to a great extent from two variables.

To start with, talking and writing (the sending parts of the correspondence procedure) are exceedingly unmistakable, and are more effectively evaluated than listening and reading (the getting parts). Furthermore, reading conduct is evaluated a great deal more oftentimes than listening conduct; that is, we are all the more frequently tried on what we read than on what we listen. Furthermore, when we are tried on material displayed in an address, by and large the address has been supplemented by readings.

Second, a hefty portion of us aren't willing to enhance our tuning in aptitudes. Quite a bit of this unwillingness results from our incomplete comprehension of the procedure—and trying to comprehend the procedure could help demonstrate to us generally accepted methods to make strides. To get the listening procedure, we should first characterize it. As the years progressed, various meanings of tuning in have been proposed. Maybe the most valuable one characterizes listening as the procedure of getting, going to, and understanding sound-related messages; that is, messages transmitted through the medium of sound. Frequently, the progressions of reacting and recalling are likewise included. The procedure travels through the initial three stages—accepting, going to, comprehension—in succession. Reacting or recollecting might also possibly take after. For instance, it might be alluring for the audience to react quickly or to recollect the message with a specific end goal to react at a later time.

Now and again, obviously, no reaction (in any event no verbal reaction) is needed. Furthermore, the demonstration of recollecting may or may not be important. Case in point, on the off chance that somebody lets you know to "watch your stride," you have no compelling reason to recollect the message after you have finished that stride. How about we take a gander at the parts—the three essential ones and the two extra ones—each one in turn? Consider the accompanying similarity between the listening procedure and the electronic mail (E-mail) framework. Assume that you are the sender of a message and I am the expected receiver.

The Process of Receiving

This stride is effortlessly caught on. You may communicate something specific to me by E-mail. It might be greatly formed and clear. You may have utilized powerful systems to sort out and bolster your message. The subject may be one of awesome enthusiasm to me. Envision promote that I both appreciate and respect you, and that I like to get E-mail from you. So, you have made a decent showing and I need to get the message. Yet, in the event that I don't turn on my PC, I won't get it. The message remains some place between your PC and mine—in the middle of sender and recipient.

Much human listening falls flat for the same reason. Receivers basically are not joined or "tuned in" to the senders. At times, the issue is a physiological one; case in point, the collector has a listening to lack because of an innate or acquired shortcoming. Then again maybe the deficiency came about because of a mischance, a sickness, or delayed introduction to uproarious commotions. At times the issue can be readdressed through the utilization of mechanical gadgets that restore listening to misfortune, or through listening devices that open up sound. Researchers and designers are continually growing new items demarked to right and help particular sorts of listening to misfortune. Keep in mind that listening and simple hearings are not the same. Hearing is the gathering of sound; listening is the appointment of importance. Hearing is, on the other hand, an important pre -essential for listening and a vital segment of the listening procedure.

The Process of Attending

How about we proceed with the E-mail relationship? When I turn my PC on, it will automatically get the message that you sent. Be that as it may, I must accomplish more: I must take care of the message if the procedure is to proceed. Maybe I got a telephone call soon after I turned my PC on and needed to move away from my work area; I don't have the foggiest idea about that you have sent a message. On the other hand perhaps I don't have a chance to check my Email that day. Assume that I am chipping away at something else when the message arrives. My PC signals that I have mail from you. I need to attend to it, yet I conclude that I will do it later. I keep on staying preoccupied on another undertaking, in any case, what's more, neglect to check the message. Later, I might erroneously "refuse it" while never understanding it. Whatever the case, I do not to take care of the message.

Human listening is regularly inadequate—or does not happen—for comparative reasons. The process of receiving the verbal ideas may happen, however the process of attending is a more critical one, and so at times people don't act upon it. At any given time, various messages go after our consideration. The boosts may be outer, for example, words talked by a speaker or imprinted on paper, or occasions happening around us. On the other hand it may be inside, for example, a due date we must meet tomorrow, a spinal pain we developed by sitting too long at the PC, or the craving strings we encounter in light of the fact that we didn't require some serious energy to eat lunch. Whatever the wellspring of the boosts, we basically can't concentrate on every one of them in the meantime. We in this manner must pick, whether deliberately or unknowingly, to go to some boosts and reject others. Three variables focus how these decisions are made.

Ross Elkins

1. *Selectivity of consideration*

Often, people choose things in which they would direct their thoughts of to prevent them from being heavily burdened by information overload. A typical case makes this point. Assume you are endeavoring to concentrate on reading a book and stare at the TV in the meantime. In spite of the fact that a few individuals claim they can do this, really both activities endure— and generally one more than the other. The material that is most captivating or fascinating will pull in your consideration. At different times, something may hinder then again aggravate your attention. Selectivity of consideration clarifies why you "liven up" or focus when something natural to you, for example, the place where you grew up or your most loved leisure activity, is said. In certainty, you may have been listening eagerly to a conversation when somebody in an alternate discussion notices your name. Instantly, the center of your consideration shifts to the discussion in which your name was said.

2. *Quality of consideration*

Consideration is not just specific; it has vitality, or quality. Consideration also obliges exertion and crave. In the illustration of reading a book and watching TV, the recipient coordinated his or her essential consideration toward either the book or the TV. Complete consideration can be given to stand out boost at a time and fundamental regard for just a predetermined number of boosts in the meantime. On the off chance that we spend a lot of vitality on an excess of boosts, we soon won't be paying consideration on any of them. We are all acquainted with flying machine mishaps that were brought on in any event to a limited extent by controllers in the tower needing to prepare a lot of data.

Consider additionally how we can be so mindful to a newspaper, a TV program, a PC, a game, event, or another person that we are absent to things around us. Watch a youthful couple in affection at some point: You'll see a decent illustration of power, or quality of consideration. Still another measure of consideration quality is the length of time that the memory of something proceeds to influence us. Quality of consideration is important.

3.   *Sustainment of consideration.*

Pretty much as consideration is resolved by selectivity and quality, it is influenced by time of sustainment. Our consideration disappears, and this is important to a comprehension of tuning in.

For instance, we can hear some out open speakers far longer than we can listen to others. Span may depend on the subject, the setting, the way the discourse is pack - matured, and on the speaker's conveyance. In any case, regardless of how well spoken and gifted the speaker, or how intriguing the content, our consideration at long last closures. On the off chance that for no other explanation, the human body obliges rest or consideration regarding other substantial needs. The psyche can just focus for whatever length of time that the body can sit still. Selectivity, quality, and sustainment focus consideration. The process of receiving and attending are essentials to the rest of the listening procedure. The third stride in that procedure is the process of understanding.

The Process of Understanding

Somebody has said, "Correspondence starts with seeing." A message may have been sent and gotten, and the collector may have taken care of the message—yet, there has been no compelling correspondence. Successful correspondence relies upon comprehension; that is, compelling correspondence does not occur until the collector comprehends the message. Understanding must result for correspondence to be compelling.

How about we come back to the E-mail similarity? Assume I got the E-mail message, "opened" it, and read it. Has compelling correspondence happened? Not so much. Despite the fact that I am able to read each expression of your message, I might not have comprehended what you implied.

There are a few conceivable purposes behind the misconception. Maybe I anticipated that the message would say something that it didn't say; my comprehension of it may therefore be more in accordance with my own desires than what it really said. We regularly hear or read what we anticipate as opposed to what was really said or composed. Then again maybe the genuine purpose of the message was "tucked away," clouded by a few different goodies of data.

What's more, I overlooked the main issue. In tuning in, the key point is once in a while missed. A laborer may tell an administrator a few things that happened while the director was out of the office. While relating every one of the occasions, the specialist notice that the manager asked that the administrator call upon his return. The manager missed this critical bit of data on the grounds that he was not "prepared" for it; that is, he was attempting to comprehend alternate parts of the message. Later, he asks the specialist for what valid reason he had neglected to let him know that his supervisor needed to see him. In any case, the laborer had told him; he simply didn't get it.

Our desires and/or our inability to get the point frequently prompt misconception. Be that as it may, the real purpose behind my misunderstanding of the E-mail I got from you was presumably something else: the words you utilized and the way in which you orchestrated them. Neither of us was fundamentally "at flaw"; we just connected diverse implications to the words. You joined one intending to those words, I connected another. We convey viably with one another just seeing that we share implications for the images—verbal or nonverbal—that we are utilizing.

With E-mail, the message is restricted to words or other visual images that speak to words. In tuning in, both verbal and nonverbal images are critical to the process of understanding.

The Process of Reacting

The listening procedure may end with comprehension, since successful correspondence and viable listening may be characterized as the precise sharing or comprehension of significance. Be that as it may, a reaction may be required—or if nothing else, supportive. Furthermore, there are distinctive sorts of reactions.

1. Direct verbal reactions. These may be talked or composed. Let us continue with the E-mail relationship. After I have gotten, went to, and comprehended the message you sent, I may react verbally. In the event that your message asked a reaction on my PC and answer to you, I may ask you for that so I can call you or come to see you, in which case I do as such. On the other hand you may have requested that I compose a position paper or consider an issue and give you some guidance, in which case I

may send a brisk E-mail reaction demonstrating that I will hit you up later.

2. Reactions that look for illumination. I may utilize E-mail to request extra data, or I may converse with you either on the phone or eye to eye. I may be immediate in my solicitation, or I might simply say, "Let me know more about it."

3. Reactions that summarize. I may say something like, "as such, what you are stating is. . . ." A rework allows the sender to concur, or to give data to illuminate the message.

4. Nonverbal reactions. Ordinarily, a nonverbal reaction is all that is required; to be sure, it may even be the favored kind of reaction. The knowing gesture of the head, an understanding grin, or a "thumbs up" may impart that the message is caught on. Reacting, then, is a type of criticism that finishes the correspondence exchange. It tells the sender that the message was gotten, gone to, and caught on.

The Process of Recalling

Remembrance of actualities is not the way to great tuning in. Yet memory is frequently a vital and necessary piece of the listening procedure. Some would go so far as to say, "On the off chance that you can't recall that it, you weren't tuning in."

This announcement is frequently untrue. Think for instance, of the times you heard a decent joke yet can't recollect that it sufficiently long to return home and let it know; or the quantity of times you have gone to the market and proved unable to keep in mind what you were requested to purchase. Furthermore, the most baffling circumstance of all—you were acquainted with someone and can't review the name five minutes after the fact. We regularly assume, "I can recollect faces, yet I can't recall names." now and again, something will "refresh" our memory, for example, hearing another joke, seeing a comparable item on the basic need store retire, or meeting another person with the same first name.

What is the relationship in the middle of memory and listening? Understanding the contrasts between short-term memory and long haul memory will help clarify the relationship. With fleeting memory, data is utilized immediately—inside of a few moments, for instance, as with a telephone number that we turn upward. Fleeting memory has a fast overlooking rate and is exceptionally helpless to interference. What's more, the measure of data that can be held is very restricted; however it differs fairly with varieties in the material to be held. Long haul memory permits us to review data and occasions hours, days, weeks—even years—after the fact. You recall, for instance, things that transpired when you were growing up, melodies you learned, and individuals you knew. You may have been uninformed of those recollections for drawn out stretches of time, and afterward the right jolt brought about you to review them. Maybe the smell of a crisply prepared pie conjured you're grandma, who used to make incredible crusty fruit-filled treats a long time ago.

Remember the old saying where people were born with just one mouth and two ears so that they could listen twice as much as they spoke? Well, there's a lot of truth in that. Listening is one of the most important and vital aspects of communication that can become abandoned and neglected. It's vital that we all know how to listen properly and how to actually glean all the information that we need to from the people we're talking to.

When you're listening to people, it's important that you're actually investing time in listening and not just investing time in building up your argument before you start talking again. Listening shows people that you're actually interested in them and actually care about what they're saying. It's so important. Just think about the people around you who don't listen to you when you speak. It's one of the most infuriating experiences that a person can go through.

So what can you do to make people feel like you actually listen to them and not just glaze over when they start to speak? Here are a few tips to be a better listener.

Hear Them:

When it comes to listening, you actually need to hear what it is they're saying. I know that might sound simple and a little too easy, but think about how much you have going on when you're listening. You have your own internal thoughts, things happening in your environment and a myriad of other distractions that are competing for your attention. So cut through the noise and actually listen to what they're actually saying to you.

No Phones:

I know that I've discussed this before, but it's so important that we need to talk about it again. Phones kill conversations and the moment someone checks or pulls out their phone, they're not paying attention to you. So, when someone is talking to you, keep your phone off or silent. People are going to hate talking to you if you're constantly checking your phone. While so many people insist that they're capable of multi-tasking, it's not true. One conversation or topic is going to take precedence and it's usually what's on the phone. So shut it off.

Digest What They're Saying:

For many people, while the other person is talking, especially when you're in a debate or argument, they take that time to think of what it is they're going to say next, not what they're being told. Rather than using this as down time to come up with what you're going to say next, actually listen and digest what it is you are being told. They have valuable insights and information that you should be more than willing to listen to. Give them a chance and open up your ears.

Listening is very important when it comes to communication. After all, communication doesn't work if we all just go around talking and there's no one to listen. So rather than talking all the time, why don't you give listening a chance and see what it is you can find out. People love to feel like they're being listened to and you're going to find that people are more willing to talk to you when you're actually listening and digesting what it is they are saying to you.

Ross Elkins

Chapter 14: Public Speaking

There comes a point in everyone's life when they're going to need to stand in front of a room full of people and talk to people who are expecting something great and impressive from them. The only sad thing about that little truth is that there are so many people out there who are absolutely horrified at the possibility of having to stand in front of people and delivering a speech to them.

Public speaking is statistically more terrifying to people than death, so how are you supposed to foster a comfortable skill set when it comes to public speaking that won't make you feel like you're going to meet a fate worse than death when you stand up? Well, I'm going to give you a few ideas that are going to help you to radically change how you approach public speaking and how you're going to succeed at any speech you're going to have to give to a group of people. So let's get started discussing how you're going to make an impression that will last and give those you're presenting to the experience of a lifetime.

Preparation:

I want you to know that this is the most crucial aspect for any presentation and you need to be completely willing to dedicate the appropriate amount of time that is required to do a good job. By knowing your information or your speech inside out, you're going to find that you're far more confident and comfortable in front of people. Know what it is you're going to be speaking about and you're going to find that the prospect of talking to all those people isn't actually as terrifying as you might think it's going to be. Know your stuff and be an expert. That's what your goal should be.

Confidence:

When you have fully prepped and are absolutely ready for the public speaking event, you might be thinking that there's still something dreadfully wrong for you. What every presenter lacks at first is confidence. By having confidence, you're projecting to the audience that what you're about to tell them is worth knowing and that you're a reliable, credible source for this information. Having that confidence is going to give you the edge so start to project it. Confidence is something that you can totally fake if you have to. If you pretend you're confident for just long enough, you'll find that your real confidence will catch up with you and give you that extra boost.

Think of it this way: confidence is what gravity is to Newton's apple...or any fruit hanging from a tree for that matter. Without doing anything, fruits will automatically fall to the ground at some point in time due to the continuous pull exerted by gravity. You can expect, without fail, that fruits will eventually fall from the branch from which they hang in due time due to gravity.

In the same manner, confidence is that special sauce or internal characteristic that ensure you're able to comfortably speak well in public each and every time. The most elaborate of preparations can still amount to nothing if you're not confident. And here's the thing: even if you're not as well-prepared as you like but if you have an overflowing abundance of confidence, you can pull off a great public speaking performance from out of your stock knowledge and experience.

You're the Expert:

What a lot of people forget when they're giving a speech or they're giving a presentation is the fact that they're the expert. You're the one who has been spending hours and hours compiling information, stories and evidence that everyone in the audience hasn't been doing. So, when you're scared that everyone in the audience is judging you, just put those fears aside. You're the expert in the room and they're listening to you for whatever information it is you can give them. So act like the expert that you are.

Just keep in mind that acting like an expert doesn't mean you have to know it all! Remember, nobody's perfect – not even you. The thing about acting like an expert is not acting like a know-it-all but having the relaxed confidence to speak in front knowing that the reason you were put there and not them is because you know more about the topic that you're going to talk about. And knowing more than them doesn't necessarily mean you'll always have to be right.

There are instances where I was rated very highly as a public speaker despite not being able to answer all the questions thrown at me by the audience. How'd I handle questions that I honestly don't know the answer to? I simply told the person who asked that it's something I haven't considered or looked into just yet and if it would alright, he or she can give me his or her contact details so I can contact him or her as soon as I have looked into his or her query. By acknowledging the things I didn't know and telling them that I would look into it, the more they respected me as an expert. Funny how acting like an expert may actually imply not acting like you know it all.

<u>Showmanship:</u>

Having a charismatic and approachable personality is vital for you to really draw in the crowds and convince them that what you're saying is important to them. So foster a need inside of them and tell them why they need this information that you're giving them. If you're presenting in front of a large group of people, don't be afraid to let your personality and your confidence show. You can tell a joke, engage them, and make them feel like they're actually getting something useful out of all of this. A great personality goes a long way in convincing people that they need to know what it is you're telling them.

Although showmanship isn't substance, it can make the substance really interesting and therefore, easier to understand. Ever wondered why many of today's liquid suspension medications for children are flavored more and more like candy? It's because tasting like it makes it easier for children to take them and because they take them, they get well.

It's the same with effectively being able to get the message across to your audience when you speak in public. The more you're able to entertain your audience, the more receptive they can be to the message you want to send across and when that happens, they'll be able to understand and get what it is you're driving at.

Of particular usefulness when it comes to showmanship in public speaking is wit and humor. Nothing else renders teaching difficult and boring stuff easier than those two. I witness this first hand almost every week in church. One of our pastors is a very funny and witty guy who can pull punch lines from the air as quickly as you can say "Peter Piper picked a peck of pickle peppers..." And considering church sermons can be just about as boring and serious as any topic can ever get, his humor makes it relatively easy for the congregation to get his main points and messages. And it's one of the reasons why our church continues to grow exponentially fast – people get the message easily.

Read the Room:

When it comes to public speaking, you should always observe your audience and know exactly how they're taking the information you're sharing. By reading the faces and the expressions of those that are in the audience, you can really tell whether or not you're being boring, slow and tedious or whether they find you credible. You want to be able to adjust to the audience and how they're enjoying the information that you're sharing with them. Getting the feedback you need in the moment gives you a lot of great chances to adapt to the situation. Make sure that you're reading your audience and that you're giving them the presentation they deserve.

Reading the room can start even before speaking engagement itself. If you have the luxury of asking the event organizer for the demographics of your audience at least a week in advance, then that would be awesome. It's because you'll have more time to evaluate what approach you should use in order to maximize the chances of the audience getting your message as you intended it to be. Then you can do more research and find out what can potentially tickle their fancy.

I experienced the great benefit of reading the room weeks in advance when I gave a talk/workshop for high school students under the outreach care of my mother-in-law. Having access to their ages and social class, I was able to do enough research about what's in or out with my target audience – high school students. As a result, I was able to give pop-culture relevant examples that they were able to relate to very easily, which helped them understand my message.

Another way you can start reading the room even before your actual speaking gig is learning how to read faces, or cold reading. It won't do you good to read the room if you're not familiar with the basic principles. By studying the art of face reading or cold-reading, you significantly increase your chances of successfully reading the room before and during your talk so you can make the necessary adjustments for effectively communicating the main ideas to them.

Public speaking is a horrifying event in the lives of so many people, but it doesn't have to be that way. You should really take a moment and take a deep breath before you really start to freak out about public speaking. With the tips that I've given you, you're going to be able to share with those around what it is you need to tell them and give the best possible performance. There's nothing scary about being an expert in what it is you've studied very hard and for a very long time. So when you're standing up there in front of your audience, make sure that you implement the suggestions I've given you and it'll be a piece of cake for you and you'll blow those fears out of the water. And as I end this chapter, allow me to share with you how I became a confident public speaker to encourage you that you can become one too.

I currently speak in front of more than 1,000 people every week. Normally, I'm given at least a week's notice as to the topic on which I'll give my short talk but there are moments when all I have is a day's notice. Scary? I know right? But would you believe me that I don't' find it scary anymore and in fact, I enjoy doing it now? Would you believe me even more if I told that I am an introvert and I had no idea many, many years ago that I would be doing this regularly and actually love it?

I used to be very shy to the point that engaging you or any other stranger was as difficult for me as begging for money at the corner of a street. That being said, how did I come to be the public speaker that I am now, and based on the feedback of many in the audience, a very good one too?

I'd really like to take the credit for getting to where I am now but the truth is, I can't. If it weren't for people who believed in me and pushed me into the spotlight, I would still be that shy, introvert adult...only many pounds lighter.

After my father died suddenly in 2000, I felt the need to try something new in my life so I joined a volunteer group in the subdivision where I live. Little did I know that introverted old me would eventually end up doing something very taboo to me – dancing in public!

To join this particular volunteer group, one had to attend a 13-week program (only one weeknight a week), which was concluded by graduation party and group presentations. Most of the people in my group were dancers and I was the only musician there. So to my chagrin, I was outvoted and the group volunteered to dance. That's how I ended up dancing in public. And I thought that was the end of my public exposure. I couldn't be more wrong.

For one reason or another that I can't fully comprehend, I was "voted" – more like pressured – to ascend to the leadership position of that group's local unit. As I reluctantly accepted, little did I know that some of its responsibilities were to give the talks in the 13-week induction program in the event that the assigned speakers can't make it. And my worst fears happened, there were a couple of nights that I had to substitute and personally give the talks. Even though the audience on average was only around 10 people at most, it is a scary proposition for a shy and introverted person like me.

Then I transferred to another group. This time, I felt I could just live a normal life and participate as a normal member. My mistake...after about a year of just resting and being an ordinary new member, that group's leadership decided to catapult me on stage. This time the average audience size was about 30 to 40 and on some really bad days (bad for me), it reached 60 people.

Something remarkably funny happened. As the months and years went by, I became comfortable with it and actually came to enjoy it. But I came to the point again where I had to transfer to another similar-natured but much bigger local group with a membership base of about 9,000. I figured, maybe this time I can really be just a regular member. After all, with a membership base that big and the group's high status in the community, I guess they have many other people more qualified than me. I was right – I was an ordinary member. But only for the first year and a half.

Soon afterward, things just happened to the point where I was back on stage but this time, in front of more than 1,000 people every time. What? And I thought it couldn't get any bigger! But there I was giving short, inspirational talks every other week or so. I was so nervous at first that I totally forgot the last and most important line, per that group's culture.

But another funny thing happened: I became more and more comfortable to the point I enjoy going up on stage in front of more than 1,000 people, which I continue to do until today.

The point of my sharing? Even if you think you're a shy introverted person, you can do well in public speaking. The important thing is to work on your confidence and practice. There can be no other way but to just have faith and show up to give your talks. Believe me, you'll eventually get the hang of it and you'll get to be very good at it in time.

Ross Elkins

Chapter 15: Learning to Trust Others (and Yourself)

There is usually no single reason that a person is unable to communicate successfully. One of the major reasons why you might be unable to communicate successfully or why you may not be able to articulate yourself is that you are unable to trust other people. You feel as though they will not understand what you have to say, or will perhaps mock it for being somehow uninteresting or unintellectual.

And for good reason! At some point in your life, maybe people close to you have betrayed the trust you've given them. You may have chosen to be vulnerable to someone and that someone betrayed that trust. It can be a corrupt politician who promised heaven and earth during the campaign period but sang a completely different tune once he or she assumed public office. It may not necessarily be a direct experience but that of someone dear to you, maybe your mom who was scammed of her life savings. Regardless, there will always be valid reasons not to trust others, even yourself.

This is obviously not a reflection of your own character. It is usually an impression you have of yourself that you project onto other people, believing that these other people that you are attempting to communicate with will believe that you are as inadequate as you believe yourself to be. The problem with this is that what you believe about yourself and others may not necessarily be the truth due to personal biases and preferences. And as we all know, deep-seated beliefs are powerful in terms of influencing our behaviors and thoughts.

A mistrust of others can also result from feeling as though they are adequate recipients of your communications. You may feel that they are in some way untrustworthy, that they are bad people or that they do not have your back. This lack of trust is natural, it is the result of bad experiences that you may have gone through in your life, or perhaps it just naturally how you are. Whatever the cause of this mistrust of others, it stops you from communicating effectively, and so must be tackled if you ever hope to start communicating in a way that will get what you are trying to say across.

It is not just others that you might not be able to trust. Very often, people that have difficulty communicating often have trust issues with themselves. Many people would be surprised by this concept. How can one mistrust oneself? After all, there is nothing more concrete than one's own personality. However, since you are reading this book, you are probably aware that this is not the case. Often there is nothing more uncertain than one's own self.

Not trusting yourself means not trusting that you will say the right things. Often when people that don't trust others to appreciate what they have to say, these same people don't believe that they have anything important to say themselves. This lack of trust results in them not saying much as all.

Chances are that you are one of these people. As you can plainly see, trust is a huge part of communication. Trusting others; trusting oneself. These things actually affect one's ability to communicate. Hence, logic dictates that if you want to communicate in a manner that is more efficient, you will have to learn trust others as well as yourself. How, though, can one learn to trust others? How can one learn to trust oneself? Such things are obviously not going to come easily, but if you are willing to work at it there are ways that by which you can overcome your issues with trust.

So why is trust a very important part of effective communications? First, if you don't trust your audience enough to be vulnerable, you won't be able to give personal examples or applications of the message you are sending in your talks. Personal examples are very powerful tools in terms of effective communications because they effectively tell your audience that you yourself have experienced the message you're giving – you have integrity. Imagine yourself giving a talk on faith, particularly why we all should have it despite the cynical world we live in. If you always give examples of how other people walked or lived in faith, your audience may wonder if you're telling the truth or if you yourself are convinced of the validity of your message. If you give personal examples of the message you're sharing to your audience, you establish integrity and authority on the subject matter, both of which can make your audience trust you and be receptive to your message. And that is the second benefit of trusting your audience enough to be vulnerable with personal examples.

When your audience trusts you and respects you as an authority or expert in the subject of your talk, you will encounter very little, if not no resistance at all to what you're discussing. With little or no resistance from the audience, they are open to consider and accept the propositions you make as you give your talk.

As you trust your audience and become vulnerable with them, they trust you back by being open and receptive to your message or be comfortable enough to ask you questions that will help them understand your message clearly. It becomes an upward spiral of continuous improvement both for you as the lead communicator and the audience as the recipient of the message. They learn from you and you learn from them how to further improve at public speaking and ultimately, at effective communications.

But if you have serious trust issues, how can you go about resolving or moving past it? The first thing that you would need to do in order to get past your issues with trust is to understand the reason behind them. Any learned man would tell you that in order to solve a problem, one must delve into and find its root cause. For it is in the understanding of a problem that one can begin to fix it a step at a time. If you don't know the main reason for it, you will never be able to end it. Sure, you can probably arrest the symptoms but more will continue popping out in different ways.

The first major cause of a lack of trust in others for you can be that you just are this way naturally. This low propensity of trust itself may have been caused by a variety of factors. A major factor that results in a low propensity to trust is the lack of positive role models while growing up. Perhaps your parents frequently let you down; perhaps you had a relative, a teacher, a friend or a sibling that you felt you could depend on that betrayed your trust by not being there when you needed them to be.

Similarly, childhood trauma is also often a cause of a lack of a desire to trust in others. It has been found in researches conducted on people who suffered abuse over the course of their lives, particularly while they were still children, are often less able to trust people than those who have not suffered any kind of abuse in their lives. Long-term emotional abuse results in you not being willing to hand your trust to other people because, growing up, all the people that you knew and who knew you would only betray your trust.

This links up with the second major cause of a lack of trust: past trauma. Past trauma, if it was serious enough, can result in some major deficiencies in one's personality. One tends to have low self-esteem, something that often results in a lack of trust in oneself. This low self-esteem usually stems from the fact that one blames oneself for the trauma one suffered. This is most often seen in rape victims, who incidentally are not very good at communicating after their trauma either.

Past trauma also often results in one treating oneself as a victim. This leads to a major shift in personality as well, which obviously affects one's communication skills. When you look at yourself as a victim, you tend to look at others as potential offenders. Your entire life becomes based around this paranoia, and mired in such paranoia you are completely unable to trust others. You are unwilling to communicate with people because you feel as though they will not understand your pain, and thus the communication will be worthless to undertake. This is a toxic personality trait. Despite your suffering, you will have to overcome this self-victimization if you can ever hope to begin communicating effectively.

The third major reason that you might not be able to trust others or yourself is, quite simply, your expectations are too high. You want people to act a certain way, and when they don't act that way, the person in question feels betrayed. This is most often seen in relationships. Unrealistic expectations, or expectations that are not overtly spoken or are unclear, will probably never be met.

People often have such unrealistic expectations about themselves as well. A man may expect himself to be a certain kind of masculine, a woman may expect herself to be dainty and soft spoken, and when these people fail to meet their expectations of themselves they begin to stop trusting themselves. They fail to communicate successfully because they feel like they are worth less than they should be. They project their expectations of themselves onto others, and since they don't meet these expectations, they will feel as though they are disappointments to other people. This will result in them not communicating successfully.

This often results in the creation of a vicious cycle. Lack of communication leads to a betrayal of trust, and the cycle goes on. The best way to cure your lack of trust is to break this cycle. You must learn to trust others. You must be wondering how you can even begin to do this, but the process is actually fairly simple. You just need to be willing to work hard at it!

Here are several ways that you can start trusting people once again:

1.   Let the fear in. You are obviously afraid of letting someone in. You must accept this fear, own it. You must make it a part of you. Once you acknowledge that you are afraid, your fear will be a tangible thing, something that can be objectively analyzed and tackled. Once it has been objectively analyzed you can do something wonderful with it: you can accept it. Acceptance of this fear is a thing so beautiful because it allows you to be comfortable with yourself, which if nothing else, would allow you to become comfortable in your own skin and begin trusting yourself for a change.

If you find this to be too much, then consider taking calculated risks. Let the fear in but put in certain contingency measures to help you manage any impact of letting your fears in and facing them. Admittedly, some fears' consequences or effects are trivial while some are quite serious. For the serious ones, do consider putting up some risk management measures. There can be no other way. Fears don't go away by simply ignoring or avoiding them. Worse, doing so can even make it grow stronger.

2.   Start cleaning up your act. People often don't communicate because they feel as though others won't think much of them. This is usually due to the fact that they don't think much of themselves. Since you are probably one of these people, how can you start to think better about yourself? Well, you need to get it together. Start being punctual, clean up your place of residence, stop sleeping so much and get some exercise. Other things you can do are to avoid alcohol and food that is not good for you. These things will boost your self-esteem, which in turn will help you feel more confident with yourself. You're probably seeing a pattern emerge here between trusting oneself and beginning to communicate better. Gaining self-confidence is the best way to begin trusting oneself, and cleaning up your act is the best way to gain confidence.

3.   Socialize. Everybody has friends, even if they just have one or two. If you want to communicate better, it is absolutely essential that you meet with these friends as much as possible. Whether they are just casual get-togethers at a local cafe or full fledged nights out partying, the more you socialize the more you're going to start trusting others. Don't have any friends at all? Join some kind of club! It doesn't have to be anything fancy,

just a book club will do. Alternatively, you can start taking dancing lessons!

The beauty of socializing or having more friends is that you have more opportunities to practice trusting people more. As your circle of friends expand with nary any incidents of broken trust, you find that trusting people becomes easier and easier. Over time, you will be able to overcome your trust issues with people and become a more effective communicator.

4.   Accept blame as well as apologies. You are not perfect, and neither is anyone else. There will be moments where you make mistakes. Accept the blame for these mistakes, and try to improve yourself so that others can trust you. Others trusting you will boost your self-confidence and can really help you communicate better! On the other hand, it is also extremely important to forgive those that have hurt you. You are invariably going to be hurt over the course of your life, and the people that hurt you are going to want to apologize. The first step to trusting others is forgiving them for their flaws.

Learning to accept both helps you grow as person and as an effective communicator. Why? Accepting blame and apologies from others is an exercise in trust. This is because when you learn to accept blame, you start trusting that people will forgive you and that they won't take your mistakes against you.

Accepting blame also helps build other people's trust in you because they see that you are open to corrections and that they can afford to be vulnerable enough to you by telling you things that they believe need to be corrected. Accepting apologies makes others trust you more and as they do, you become more comfortable trusting them too. It becomes an upward spiral of ever improving abilities to trust for both you and others around you.

5.   Learn to love yourself. Everyone is self-deprecating to some degree, so you should feel guilty for criticizing yourself. However, drowning your inner consciousness in a sea of negativity is not exactly healthy. It will sap your self-confidence and leave you feeling worthless. Balance out the negativity with the occasional smidgen of positivity. Find praiseworthy characteristics to your personality or your physical appearance and think to yourself, "This is a good thing about me, I appreciate this aspect of myself." This will help you become more confident which will in turn help you open up and communicate better!

Yes, humility is important for improvement but humility doesn't need to become self-loathing. Being humble enough to accept your mistakes and committing to do things right the next is actually loving yourself because by doing so, you put yourself in a position to become a much better person, a more trusting one and an even more effective communicator.

6.   Don't take things so seriously. Work is work. It is important, but it is only one aspect of your life. So are your romantic relationships. Certain aspects of your life often leave you feeling enraged. You need to overcome these strong emotions if you can ever hope to achieve any significant boost in your confidence whatsoever. Learn to control your anger, your sadness and your impatience. Learn not to take things so seriously and you will definitely start feeling like your communication levels are improving when they aren't impaired by powerful emotions!

7.   Take it a step at a time. This is possibly the single most important thing that you can do in order to start communicating in a more effective way. Just saying hello to somebody is a significant step. Being able to trust someone with the keys to your home is a major step. However, you should always take this journey a step at a time. Focus on opening up about yourself piece by piece. Tell someone your favorite color, a dream you had last night, what you did or didn't like about your parents. Before you know it, you will be communicating with the best of them.

Chapter 16: Learning to be Honest

Honesty is perhaps just as important a factor in one's communication skills as trust. These two are, in many ways, intertwined, not least of all because one almost always leads into the other.

Miscommunication is a blanket term that can be used to describe any kind of communication that is in any way faulty or dysfunctional. Any type of communication that causes problems is essentially miscommunication. One of the biggest forms and causes of miscommunication is dishonesty. Hence, honesty and a lack thereof must be considered an essential form of communication as a whole.

In order to understand what honesty is, and how one can attempt to be honest in general, one must also strive to understand dishonesty as well. You must understand that there are several forms of dishonesty, and several variations of these forms. Dishonesty is the absence of honesty in communication, and this term can be applied to many, many things.

Lying is perhaps the most pervasive form of dishonesty in human society. You can lie for a variety of reasons. Perhaps there is financial gain in the lie, perhaps there is upward social mobility. You might lie in order to avoid a punishment for something that you have done, in which case you would claim that it was not you who did it. We lie to others for a lot of reasons, but it also very important to realize that we also lie to ourselves.

How exactly do we lie to ourselves? We tell ourselves that something we are doing is not wrong, that it is excusable. We also lie to ourselves to justify our mistreatment of other people. We can lie to ourselves and tell ourselves that we are actually good at communicating, that it is everyone else who is at fault.

Therein lies the fundamental importance of honesty within the realm of communication. A lack of honesty is perhaps the single greatest impediment to the improvement of your communication skills. Hence, it is pretty clear that in order to communicate better, you're going to have to learn how to be honest.

Being Honest With Others

Communicating successfully means being honest, but it also means knowing *how* to be honest. Remember, a lot of the time people don't want honesty. They want you to deceive them in order to make them feel better about themselves. It is absolutely essential that you humor them in this regard. After all, if you were not looking particularly good on a certain day, would you want someone to be blunt and honest and tell you look ugly? Perhaps you were unable to shower because you woke up late. Perhaps you did not have time to look in the mirror in the morning. Whatever the case may be, you are not going to feel good about yourself after someone heartlessly tells you that you don't look good, no matter how honest they were being.

Yet, honesty is an important part of communication. You would not lie about owing someone money or about whether you are capable of a certain task or not. Where then is the line drawn? Human suffering, of course. You do not lie when the lie will cause someone else pain, and you do lie when someone's happiness or self-esteem is at stake. However, this line is a difficult one to see sometimes. In order to help you maintain a level of honesty that is conducive to healthy and efficient communication, here are a few tips:

1. Start small: chances are you are not a very honest person. This is not a reflection of your character; perhaps you've been brought up in a way that you had to include small falsehoods into your everyday speech. If this is the case, it's best not to bite off more than you can chew, since you won't know just how honest to be and what type of

honesty would best suit a certain situation. Start becoming honest by, for example, telling your friends that you can't make it to a get together because you don't feel like it rather than lying and saying that you are feeling under the weather.

2. Don't put honesty off for later: if you have become used to lying, even small white lies, these falsehoods will have become easy by now. They will have become the easy way of getting out of difficult conversations. If you are looking to start communicating more effectively, honesty should be high on your list of priorities, and thus these difficult conversations must be had. However, since they are not the easy way out you might feel like procrastinating and putting the honesty off for later. This is unacceptable. Face your dishonesty like a man and get the truth off your chest. Do this often enough and you will soon find your communication skills will have improved drastically!

3. When white lies are okay: there are obviously certain situations where white lies are okay. A white lie is essentially a lie that does not majorly deceive somebody and thus will not result in anybody getting hurt. However, it is important to know just when and where white lies are for the greater good, as telling them too often and for personal gain is just another form of

miscommunication and is detrimental to your progress. Whenever honesty is both unnecessary and would probably end up hurting the other person, it's probably better to keep that information to yourself and tell a white lie instead. For example, if your partner asks you if you think she is obese, fat, chubby or whatsoever. She is most likely feeling insecure because of the unfair beauty criteria imposed on her by the mass media, so making a little white lie is the most appropriate and right thing to do.

4. Don't be too blunt: there is a difference between honesty and bluntness. For example, if your friend wants an honest opinion on the spray tan he is using, saying "It looks terrible!" is very blunt and would probably hurt his feelings. Try to be subtle in your honesty in this regard. Instead of saying outright that the spray tan looks terrible, subtly suggest that it doesn't suit them for some reason or the other. This way, you are being honest, as you have been asked to be, but at the same time you are safeguarding that person's feelings and ensuring that you don't hurt them. Remember, blunt honesty may not be as bad as dishonesty, but it is dysfunctional communication at best and so should be worked on in order to start communicating in more effective manner.

5. Remember the importance of apologizing: there is no shame in having been dishonest, even if your dishonesty stretched over a long period of time, as long as you are now taking steps to ensure that you are no longer dishonest. If you have been dishonest for a long time, your natural escape mechanism after having made a mistake will probably be lying in order to make the person you have wronged either believe that the mistake was not your fault or that it was somehow justified. This is obviously the wrong thing to do. The right thing to do would be to tell the truth and apologize for your mistake. You may think that this would get you into trouble, but in general people appreciate that you respected them enough to be honest and apologize for what you have done. Additionally, you will not have to go through the guilt that stems from having deceived someone!

6. Keep the option of private honesty in mind: often, people are dishonest simply because they are too embarrassed to admit their problem in a public forum. There are also certain situations where being honest in a public forum is simply not a good thing to do, situations where the honesty that you must display is too embarrassing for the person it pertains to. For example, if you have a friend whose significant other is cheating on them, being honest

with them and telling them about it in public would probably be an extremely embarrassing experience for them. Similarly, saying loudly and in public that your friend has something between their teeth would also be embarrassing, despite the fact that you were just being honest. Being honest in private is the preferred form of honesty in these situations. Remember, honesty is a good thing when it is helping the other person, so privately being honest with people about things that might hurt them is an important part of being tactful.

7. Honesty requires explanation: there are obviously certain situations where honesty is absolutely necessary. An example of such a situation is the aforementioned situation where you have a friend whose significant other is being unfaithful to them. In such situations it is usually important to be both discreet and reveal your honesty to the person in private as well as explain the reason for your honesty. Make it absolutely clear that you are not being honest to hurt them; you are being honest because you want to be a good person and tell them what they need to know. Honesty must never be used as a weapon and you shouldn't use it in this manner.

8. Honesty with an emphasis on the positive is a good thing. People often ask for advice, and in the vast majority of

situations would appreciate it if you were honest while providing the advice. This is going to put you in a lot of situations where you have to be honest with the other person and make a negative comment about their appearance or a project that they might be working on. Remember that, although they were asking for honesty, they weren't asking for rudeness or to be put down. When you have to say something negative for the purpose of being honest, try to pad this negativity with a lot of positivity. Tell the person who has asked for your honest opinion that your opinion is a negative one, but it is not their fault or it is a natural part of being at the skill level they are at. In all things, making people feel good about themselves is an essential part of communicating successfully. Since honesty is such an important part of communicating in an effective manner, this applies to this situation as well.

9. Don't always assume you're right. Whenever you give somebody an honest opinion, remember that that's exactly what it is, an opinion. Just because you're being honest about the way you feel about something does not mean that what you are saying automatically becomes fact. On the contrary, it is just another honest opinion. People will either choose to take it seriously or they won't

and you will have to respect their decision either way. Many people make the serious blunder of getting offended whenever an opinion that they provide is not acted on or taken seriously. Nobody owes it to you to take your opinion seriously. You are being honest for yourself in such situations, and other people are free to accept your honesty and appreciate you for it but not act on it.

10. Always think about what you are about to say. Do unto others what you expect for yourself, or so the saying goes. This is perhaps the most basic rule in the entire world of communication. Think before you talk. Whenever you are talking to somebody, mull over the words that you are going to say before actually saying them. Ask yourself "Are these words harsh or blunt? Are you being dishonest without realizing it?" All in all, just try your best to speak to people the way you would like to be spoken to yourself. As long as you follow this one simple rule, you will find that soon your communication skills will have improved and you will have automatically started to become a lot more honest when it is needed and it counts!

Ross Elkins

Chapter 17: How to Communicate Better in a Relationship

Communication is an important part of each and every aspect of our lives. From our work life to our social lives, the way we communicate dictates everything from our social mobility to our status at work and any potential promotions we might receive. However, in no aspect of our lives is communication more important than in our relationships.

Relationships are bonds between you and other people. Such two person bonds simply cannot exist if a large amount of communication does not take place between them. After all, it is this communication that helps us form these bonds in the first place and find common ground that serves as the basis of the relationship.

Relationships include those that we are born with, such as our relationships with our parents, as well as those that we choose to become part of, such as romantic relationships and friendships. In all of these relationships, proper communication is absolutely necessary.

Often, these relationships fail specifically due to the fact that communication between the two vested parties isn't working. Forms of miscommunication such as lying, angry outbursts and other similar methods of communication, which really don't get any kind of positive message across harm our relationships. They can often damage a relationship in ways that are entirely irreparable.

Hence, it is probably clear to you by now that in order to maintain the relationships you are a part of, you are going to have to start communicating more effectively. You may be wondering how you can start communicating better or how you can improve your relationship by creating a dialogue between you and the person you are in a relationship with. There are several ways that you can do this.

Spend Time Together

Spend time together. Don't just sit in front of the TV and watch repeats of boring shows. Don't just sit next to each other, superficially together, but actually buried deep into the digital world of your smartphone. Take some time out to be together and actually talk. Listen to what the other person has to say, give your input about whether you think what they are saying is right or wrong. Listen, respond, argue, talk and communicate!

This helps in a lot of ways. First of all, you learn how to effectively get what you are saying across to the person you love because they react to what you say and how you say it. You can modify the way you say certain things and avoid saying other things altogether in order to start communicating in a way that is more effective and efficient. You also learn how other people communicate. If you have difficulty communicating in an efficient manner, you need to realize that the best way to start communicating effectively is to listen to how other people communicate. You can apply the communication techniques that other people use in your own communications. Spending time with the people you are in relationships with is a great way to improve your communication skills overall and helps keep the relationships healthy to boot.

Leave Your Ego at the Door

A major cause of miscommunication between two partners, friends or relatives is that their individual egos cause too much strife and result in the wrong things being said. People tend to take things personally. Certain comments seem to make partners in a relationship feel as though their sense of self worth is somehow being questioned or lowered.

You need to realize that everything is not about you. Certain comments made by your significant other or friend might leave you feeling slighted, but you need to realize that it is highly unlikely that they said what they said in order to hurt you.

This is one of the most common forms of miscommunication between two people who are in some form of a relationship. The presence of an overly large ego usually results in one of the parties taking a certain comment the wrong way. The fact of the matter is that a relationship is a two-way road. If you feel like something your partner or friend has said has somehow offended you, you need to talk to them about it.

The gist is, get over yourself. If you are hurt by something, communicate about it. Don't get trapped in your ego and think that the other person somehow owes it to you to figure out what they have done or said in the first place. If you want to start communicating better, you need to start communicating yourself, your ego be damned.

Avoid Resentment Stemming From Lack of Communication

You may feel that in certain situations your partner or friend says or does something that offends you in some way. Perhaps they said something about the way you look, perhaps they commented on a project that you were undertaking and subtly criticized it. Maybe they did so intentionally, maybe they didn't. Since you have difficulty communicating in an effective manner, something tells me that you won't be communicating your feelings to them any time soon.

There are probably quite a few reasons for this. First and foremost, you may feel as though your opinions are not noteworthy. You may assume that whatever they said you deserved, probably as a result of your low self-esteem. You might also believe that you cannot communicate the way you are feeling simply because your significant other will not understand what you are trying to say. Perhaps you feel as though they will think you weak for getting upset over something so ostensibly, small. Being brought up with a certain sense of masculinity can often do that to a man.

However, it is very important that you realize that your lack of communication in this regard is detrimental to your relationship. Your significant other will never know that a particular comment hurt you and would repeatedly make the same mistake again. You will never be able to ascertain whether the things they had said were intentionally hurtful or if they had simply made a mistake. Eventually, hurt will turn to resentment and the relationship will subsequently deteriorate past the point of reparation. All of this can be prevented if you just take that brave first step and let your significant other know that what they did or said hurt you.

This Is Not a Competition

Over the course of any relationship, you and your significant other, or you friend, are definitely going to argue. This is not a possibility. It is an absolute certainty. Two people coming together in a relationship will almost certainly have a difference in opinion, which will almost certainly result in a clash of personalities.

This is nothing to worry about. It is simply a natural part of every human relationship. After all, pretty much every human being is fundamentally different. Even if you find somebody who shares a lot of your opinions and tastes, there are going to be moments, several of them in fact, in which you disagree, and these moments will most often lead to arguments. In this manner, arguments are actually quite healthy. They help you and your significant other get past these fundamental differences and ease the tension that is invariably present.

Hence, argument is a fundamental part of communication. However, how you approach argument is extremely important. In too many situations, couples approach arguments in the worst way possible. They treat them like competitions. Your relationship is a bond that has been created for the purpose of mutual growth. Your arguments are not competitions that you can win. Listen to what your significant other has to say and get them to listen to what you have to say. This is how you are going to start improving your communication skills and your relationship as well.

Respect opinions

Chances are, you are a person with strong opinions. You believe that Coke tastes better than Pepsi, basketball is the greatest sport in the world or that Radiohead is the greatest band in the world. You believe that a certain football team is better than another football team because one has better players. You need to realize that although your opinions are certainly extremely important, they are also just what they are, opinions.

Opinions are what you believe is true about subjective topics. Music, taste and sports are all subjective. What this means is that just because you have an opinion does not mean that it is necessarily true. It does not mean that your significant other, friend or any other person that you are currently in a relationship with is going to share your opinions.

In order to improve communications with your loved ones, it is essential that you are open to their opinions, and are accepting of the fact that they may not share yours. Maintaining an attitude of superiority based on your own opinions is going to seriously impact your ability to communicate in a manner that is effective and efficient.

Mind What You Say and How You Say It

Words are important. They possess weight and they affect their recipients. Your words can cut and they can heal, they can prop people up or shoot them down. All in all, words are weapons as well as medicine. Weapons can be used to defend people, and medicines in the wrong dosage can kill people.

What all of this means is that you should think about what you say before you say it. By saying something, no matter how insignificant it is to you, you might be hurting your significant other. The best policy in this situation is to imagine how you would feel if somebody said something similar to you. Don't adopt a high and mighty point of view and pretend that nothing you say is hurtful. Be honest with yourself and realize where you are going wrong in the way you are communicating with your significant other.

Apart from what you say, you should also be careful about how you say it. This ties in with the previous chapter regarding honesty as well. Often, a lot of things simply must be said. If your girlfriend is being too clingy and is not giving you enough time yourself, you definitely need to tell her. This is important because the two of you need to spend a significant amount of time together. Not letting her know that something she is doing is bothering you will end up poisoning the relationship, as you will begin to resent her for doing something you dislike.

At the same time, it is very important to understand that the way you tell her that what she is doing annoys you is also very important. Your tone, the way you approach the topic; all of these are an essential part of the message you send. If you are overly harsh, it could end up harming your relationship and making the situation worse than it already was.

Focus on a Thing at a Time

Discussion and communication is essential to the health of a relationship, this much you probably already know. Often, when communication has begun to wane between two people who are in some sort of a relationship, it is important to sit down and have a discussion and talk about anything and everything that each of you feels is affecting the relationship.

This is a great way to get past certain things that either of you might find annoying, hurtful, or to discuss things that each of you find pleasant. This allows you to humanize each other, to gain a deeper level of understanding regarding each other's likes and dislikes as well as what each of you wants from this relationship.

However, whilst having a discussion, it is also important to realize that you cannot let the conversation meander through a variety of topics. You need to be concise and be focused. The thing is, communication is great. It is literally the only way to let other people know what you want. However, communication without a single focus can often lead to the problem at hand never being discussed properly. Hence, when you talk to your significant other, it is important that the two of you maintain a single topic of discussion until that topic has been exhausted after which you can move on to the next topic.

Focus on what's Similar

While you are communicating with your significant other, you will come across a huge amount of differences between the two of you. This has been mentioned before in this chapter in the section regarding arguments. Arguments are certainly where a lot of discrepancies in personality and opinion will lead.

However, in order to successfully communicate with your significant other and successfully continue your relationship, if in fact that is what you wish to do, it is very important that you try your best not to focus on these arguments alone.

Everybody has his or her differences. However, the fact that the two of you are in a relationship means that you obviously have some similarities as well. There are probably positive aspects to your relationship along with the negative. Otherwise you wouldn't be in a relationship in the first place.

In order to communicate better, you need to see past the negative aspects of your relationship. Focus on the positives as well, and you will surely see an improvement in the way you communicate.

Don't Make Assumptions

Communication is how you find out what your significant other is feeling or thinking. However, it is extremely common for people to simply assume that someone feels a certain way about something when in reality the opposite is true. Obviously, the person that has made the assumption has no idea how the other person feels. Yet they feel as if they can ascertain their entire emotional profile from a single expression they make, or their tone of voice or loudness level as they speak a single word.

Never make assumptions about what somebody else is feeling. Never make assumptions about what somebody meant by saying a particular thing. This is one of the greatest impediments to effective communication because it is literally the opposite of effective communication. Making assumptions means that there is a complete lack of any form of communication whatsoever.

If you find yourself making an assumption regarding how your significant other is behaving, just approach them and talk to them. Communicate. Ask them why they said what they said, or if they really feel the way you think they do about something that you said or did.

Communication is all about connection. Don't sever the connections that you can enjoy because of your ego. Making assumptions often leads to frustration simply because you cannot be completely sure about what the other person is truly thinking unless you ask them. Do yourself a favor. Save yourself the frustration and just communicate with them in the first place.

Accept Your Mistakes

This book is meant for humans communicating with other humans. Chances are, you are a human. In fact, I am certain that you are one. Humans make mistakes. It is what makes us so beautifully tragic and endearing at the same time. Since you are human, chances are that you're going to make more than a few mistakes over the course of your life. This does not make you evil; it just means that you are just as flawed as the rest of us.

A common mistake made in communicating with others is a refusal to accept blame, not acknowledging that there are certain flaws inherent in all of us. Maybe you have a tendency to drink too much, perhaps you have anger issues that you need to sort through, perhaps you are too sensitive and people simply don't know what to say around you. In a relationship, these flaws are going to get in the way of effective communication. However, what is more detrimental to effective communication is a refusal to acknowledge these flaws.

When you refuse to accept your mistakes and flaws you become defensive, you attempt to victimize yourself and, in doing these things, you build a wall around yourself, a wall that prevents you from communicating with your significant other or from them communicating with you. In order to begin communicating more effectively, learn to accept yourself for who you are, acknowledge your mistakes and try to work on them.

No Interruptions

There is nothing that disturbs the flow of a river more than stones thrown into it at regular intervals. Although the stones may seem insignificant, over a period of time they can actually begin to alter the way the river flows. A large enough build up of stones can stop the flow of a river entirely.

In this analogy, the river is communication and the stones are interruptions. Interruptions are the bane of good communication, because people tend to get into a flow when they are talking about something and unnecessarily interrupting them results in them getting distracted. They therefore become unable to articulate what they were trying to say as efficiently as they were doing before. This is very frustrating, which leads to resentment, which leads to a further breakdown in communication.

Often, interjections in conversation are a welcome thing. As long as they are positive interjections that tell your significant other that you are actually listening to them, like statements of agreement, suggestions and so on, they can actually lead to an improvement in communications between your significant other and yourself.

Interruptions, on the other hand, usually occur during an argument or a discussion of flaws or mistakes. If your partner is trying to communicate something, you need to hear them out all the way. Listen to everything they have to say, understand what it is they are saying. Finally, when they are done, you can respond.

Prefer Face-to-Face Interaction

We live in a largely digital world. The vast majority of human interaction now takes place through the use of technology. We see each other via video calling apps, we listen to each other over the phone, we stay in touch through social media but by far the most popular method of communication these days is text messaging.

Text messaging is ostensibly an improved version of letter writing. However, in writing a letter, tears can fall on the page. Handwriting can describe the emotions of the writer, and a personal touch is always added. Text messaging, like all modern forms of communication, is largely sterile. Almost no emotion can be displayed via texts, which leads to a lot of assumptions and guesswork, which in turn leads to frustration and a breakdown in communication.

Hence, it is absolutely essential that you communicate with your partner face to face. Face to face interaction is how human beings were always meant to communicate. It is important that you place emphasis on face to face interaction because it is only when meeting someone face to face can you see their expressions, truly hear their voices and the tones in which they speak completely free of all forms of electronic modulation.

Communication is easy over electronic devices. You just type something out and send it. The vast majority of cues that we get from face to face interaction are not there. It is only through attempting the difficult way, the right way, can you improve your communication skills.

Pay Attention

This section is very similar to the one regarding not interrupting. The thing is, people want to communicate. Your significant other wants to tell you about her day. She wants to tell you about her hopes and her dreams, she wants you to know what she thinks of you and she wants to know what you think of her as well. If there is a problem in communication and it's not with the other person, it's probably with you and is most probably caused by not paying attention to what the other person is saying.

People want to feel gratified. They want to feel as if the things that they are saying matter and that they are being listened to. They want to feel like their words mean something to the person they are speaking to. As you already know, interruptions are absolute no go areas. At the same time, you cannot simply be talking to your significant other and not listening to them speak.

People very frequently begin to daydream when a conversation is underway. When it is not your turn to speak, you probably begin to think about other things because you feel as if what is being said is, for some reason, not important. You need to pay attention, and you need to listen. If you want to improve the way you communicate, it is absolutely essential to do this in order to make the other person feel as though their opinions matter.

Honesty is Key

You simply can't have a relationship without honesty. After all, how can you even hope to trust somebody that lies to you? Similarly, you cannot expect other people to trust you and communicate with you when your communication with them involves deception and dishonesty.

Often, dishonesty involves not lying but simply not being straightforward about what it is you want out of the relationship. If your significant other wants to talk about getting married and you aren't ready, you might avoid the topic or change the subject. This is a terrible way to go about it. Eventually you are going to have to tell your significant other what you think of this relationship.

Additionally, not all dishonesty is evil. There are such things as white lies, after all. These small lies can be about anything, from sexual performance to what you think about the other person's parents. Remember, honesty is important in a relationship. No matter what it is, if you feel you have to lie about to save yourself from going through uncomfortable conversations then you must not lie; you must tell the truth.

However, keep in mind that you shouldn't be honest in all situations. As has been stated in the chapter regarding honesty, if the lie you are telling will keep your loved one from experiencing unnecessary pain, then you are justified in your deception. Do not make a habit of dishonesty, as it is a huge impediment to successful communication.

Do Not Delay Communication

If you feel like something is wrong, you absolutely have to talk about it. Unless there are circumstances that mean that you simply cannot speak to your significant other at all, there is no reason to delay communication.

Once you start experiencing a problem with any aspect of your life, it starts to create an aura around you. This aura is one of tension and stress, and it will almost certainly affect your relationship as well. Your significant other will be unwilling to communicate with you because they will feel as though they are causing this aura.

You absolutely cannot let this happen. If something is wrong, it is essential that you tell your significant other. Let them know whether they are the cause of the problem or not, and tell them as soon as possible. Otherwise your problem will fester into something that might result in the end of your relationship.

Learn to Forgive

You cannot communicate with your partner if you feel as though they he/she has wronged you. However, you need to realize that he/she makes mistakes and has flaws just like you do. The section regarding acknowledging your own flaws also means that you need to acknowledge the flaws of others and be willing to forgive them for it.

Holding on to grudges means you will begin to see everyone as an enemy. This is going to greatly impact your communication skills in a negative way.

Savor It

There are many people out there that attempt to rush through conversations because they feel that it is something that they need to get over with as soon as possible. This is actually the opposite of what you should do.

Speaking quickly will technically finish a lot of the conversation faster than it would otherwise, but it will leave almost nothing said properly. This is worse than a lack of communication. This is miscommunication.

You need to speak slowly. Encourage your partner to do so too. Savor the words you say and make them count. Doing so will help you communicate like never before.

Ross Elkins

Chapter 18: How to Communicate Better in a Business Environment

Communication is a process of conveying your ideas and your point of view to other individuals. In this regard, communication is not just a one sided process, since it also includes listening to any ideas, problems and suggestions that others might have and then acting on what has been said. This is an essential factor that is required if you ever hope to function in a business environment.

You may now be wondering, what exactly is a business environment? Well a business environment is a term generally used to describe situations that fall within a company's operations. This includes a pretty much every aspect of a business's dealings. Clients, suppliers, the competition, the owners, changes in the legal framework of businesses and market trends all constitute the business environment.

Since there are so many entities that must be interacted with within the business environment, it's no wonder that communication is such an important asset to the successful businessman or corporate climber. Communication is perhaps the single most indispensable component of the business environment in this way. If one is unable to communicate successfully, how can one fix this and begin to communicate in a manner that is more successful and efficient? How can one improve communication skills pertaining to the business environment? Here are some of the steps involved in this process:

Know Your Audience

For starters, you should know the audience you're addressing, because once you know your audience, it makes getting your ideas and opinions across much easier. Different audiences require different styles of communication.

A more reserved audience will require a more reserved manner of speaking. In general, corporate clients tend to be quite efficient in this respect. They demand a sense of austerity, which means that during your presentation, you need to be especially formal while addressing an audience.

Then, of course, there are situations where being informal and jovial is very important. If you are in a managerial position, you will often have to communicate with your employees in a manner that is informal in order to make you appear approachable to them.

Hence, it is clear to see that the way you communicate is very important depending on what kind of audience you are facing.

Different Methods of Communication

There are two ways of communicating

- Verbal communication: This includes all manner of speech as well as written communication. This includes all of the skills that help in sharing ideas, views and discussions, cooperation and one's ability to complete tasks at hand that involve speaking or writing skills.

- Non-verbal communication: Non-verbal communication includes one's posture, body language and gestures. Also, how one dresses and presents him or herself in front of an audience matters. A lot of non-verbal communication is unintentional; it is the direct result of one's particular personality. However, you can attempt to change this by intentionally adding non-verbal cues to the way you speak, such as adopting authoritative postures and being aware of body language.

Usage of Oral and Written Communication

Oral communication is usually used in a discussion of ideas and in problem solving. In professional environments, presentation matters a lot. Hence, this explains why staffs are trained thoroughly to be able to fluently present to their audience.

Written communication is used for sending letters to clients, suppliers and other business officials. This should always be professional.

Usage of electronic forms of communication

Electronic forms of communication play an integral and important role in any kind of business environment. Electronic forms of written communication are either emails or faxes. In simpler terms, these forms of communication are any type of communication that can be transmitted digitally. While you are in an office environment, your job will be to interpret loads and loads of information that will be seeding through several sources. The information will be reaching you manually or digitally. It is quite easy to single out the information that is received manually, however, the same cannot be said for the information received digitally so the person working in the business environment needs to make sure that whatever information is chosen, it's correctly written and professionally presented.

Language used for written communication

Communication is known as the process of delivering a message or a speech through several different ways: ideas, thoughts, emotions and sometimes even body language. Considering how you are in a business environment, the language you should be using to communicate should be a language that everyone can understand. Remember when you are writing to someone, they don't have the clues of seeing you or your body language, so your written communication should always be clear. Read it through before sending it.

Tones Used for Written Communication There are three styles and tones used for written communication that may vary while keeping the audience in mind. These are:

1. COLLOQUIAL LANGUAGE: This term is used to refer to any sort of language that is extremely informal. It includes street slang and localized colloquialisms. A good example of colloquial language is cockney English, which is a localized form of English found in urban London. Such language is never acceptable in a business environment. Avoid slang at all costs.

2. FORMAL LANGUAGE: Formal language is the most respectful language one can use in written communications. Attention should be paid to spelling and grammar. Fillers such as "you know" and "like" are

avoided, and attempts are made to articulate what one is attempting to say in a manner that is clear. Formal language is usually used in the business environment while talking to potential clients or to levels of management.

3. INFORMAL LANGUAGE: Informal language is a midway point between formal language and colloquial language. It is often difficult to see the difference between informal language and language that is more colloquial. In general, informal language consists of words that are universally recognized, yet the language is not quite as austere as formal language. Within a business environment, informal language is generally used to converse with members of the team you are in charge of, or members of upper management that don't greatly outrank you. This more casual approach denotes closeness to the people you are writing to.

Keeping the seven C's of communication in mind

The most essential part of written communication is to keep the seven C's of communication in mind before writing anything. The seven C's of communication are as follows:

1. CLEAR: The written text should not be vague and should be perfectly understandable to the reader. The language used

should be as transparent as possible, with every attempt being made to use the simplest language that can be used for the purposes of keeping the information that is being recorded as easy to interpret as possible.

2. CONCISE: Since business officials and clients do not have free time on their hands, the writer must keep the text as short as possible without missing out important details. Do not use fluff words, do not over express details or describe things more than is necessary. Write what you need to write, describe if absolutely necessary, and move on. The people you are writing to don't have time to read through volumes of information.

3. CONCRETE: Any information mentioned in the written text should be backed up with evidence or be solid. Try as much as you can to leave out any information that is not one hundred percent correct. There will obviously be situations where you simply will not be able to ascertain whether a piece of information is correct or not, but bear in mind that what you write represents the company view. In cases where you have to use guesswork, make it absolutely clear that the information is not confirmed and state concisely why you included it in your report.

4. CORRECT: Only correct information should be added to the text. If the writer is unsure about whether the information is

correct or not then he or she should not add it or should add a disclaimer.

5. COHERENT: The sentences should be properly structured and coherent. Do not meander and do not digress. Since this is a professional report, exercise a measure of professionalism.

6. COMPLETE: The information present in the text should be complete with all the necessary details mentioned.

7. COURTEOUS: The most important factor is to keep the tone formal and courteous. Showing respect is one of the most important parts of business culture, so if you are in doubt about something you are writing about, be courteous.

Presentation of written text

The written text should be coherent as mentioned above and organized in such a manner so that there is no doubt left in the reader's mind. Everything should be written in a clear concise manner. The structuring of the written text should be as below:

1. Introduction

2. Information

3. Conclusion.

The entire written text should be written in a courteous tone, giving respect to the reader.

Accuracy of Grammar, Punctuation and Spellings

When the writer is writing a written communication, the correct use of grammar, punctuation as well as the correct use of spellings is extremely important. If the readers end up finding any sort of grammatical mistakes or any shady use of punctuation, chances will be that they will stop reading what's important and dwell on the errors. It is highly necessary that the standard of work that is being done is impeccable and up to the international standards. It should not contain mistakes. Do keep in mind that a mistake can cost you a loss so make sure whatever you are writing is hundred percent accurate and to the point.

As you will be writing in English, try to make it as clear as possible and avoid using complicated jargon unless you know the recipient will understand it. Use the type of English that is extremely simple and easy to understand to everyone who has basic reading skills.

Proof read your work

Proof reading is another very important factor in written communication. By proof reading, you will be making sure that whatever you have written is written perfectly and there aren't any unnecessary mistakes present in your work. The perfect way to proof read your work is to read it aloud, although that isn't always practical.

POINTERS FOR VERBAL COMMUNICATION

Simple use of language

The presenter should always keep in mind the audience he or she is presenting to and the factors that matter are age, gender and the literacy level of the audience. The use of simple language is the best way to present to audience of all ages, literacy level and genders as they will find it easy to understand and there will be no doubts left in their minds.

Importance of contribution

Contributing is also a really important part of verbal communication. Whenever there is a verbal communication is going on, make sure you contribute whenever you feel the time is right for you to pitch in. Do keep in mind that you are not just there to be heard. Listening to others while they deliver their opinions is also very necessary because if you are not paying attention to what your colleagues are saying, you will be completely lost and your contribution will be less valuable.

Keep a professional body language

Body language is as important in verbal communication as anything else. No one would be willing to take you seriously if your body language lacks the touch of a professional, so always make sure that your body language is professional while you are communicating verbally. Keep your posture rigid and if you are planning on moving around, make sure you do it for a purpose. For example, pointing things out on a chart may require you to move. Apart from the entirely professional body language, you can also use positive hand gestures to show how you are fully dedicated to the work you are doing.

Taking Notes

For verbal communication, taking notes is a very important factor. It shows that you are an active listener and also helps in contribution and makes it obvious that you are paying attention to the presenter, which is considered a highly professional attitude.

Ross Elkins

Chapter 19: How to Pitch an Idea

To create and refine an idea is the main goal. Just having an idea does not help. It does not create any success; it builds nothing further from the idea. Ideas bounce off other ideas. That's the way communication works. People tend to become so smug when they get an idea, their ego takes over and convinces them not to build the idea any further which is always a mistake. Bounce your ideas off others, as combined efforts always pay off.

Considering the fact that 100 ideas can bounce off of a single idea that gives you a lot of scope for improvement. Planning, sketching out the idea, building and constructing takes time and require patience. The foundation of an idea can be easily dismissed and discouraged if you can't back it up by being able to answer questions. A vague idea is fine as long as the specific details are worked out and followed up on. Before presenting a new idea, imagine the questions that will be asked and be ready for them with solid answers that back up your ideas.

You need to know what problems your idea will be solving and to whose benefit the idea is. Selling an idea to others, they will want to know why they should consider the idea and your communication at this stage is vital. Thus, having the idea isn't enough. Have answers ready for those who doubt the idea.

The scope of an idea

The bigger the idea is, the more people it may affect. You can use charts to demonstrate your idea in a clearer manner, so that others can see the same vision. That helps considerably in the negotiation process and aids your communication of that idea.

Working on a chart will keep your team informed and also helps you to keep everyone in the picture as the job proceeds. It also pinpoints difficulties in others tasks. You will find this aids communication with other workers and gives them a very clear picture of the progress of the idea in action.

Apart from the idea itself, one must also focus on communicating this idea to potential clients, or anybody that would be interested in the idea that you have. Being shy or reserved is simply not an option in this situation, you will have to be assertive and you will have to get your message across if you want your pitch to be successful.

The power to the idea

You will have to list down the required recipients of your pitch. This list is cut down to two criteria: People who have power to actually put your idea into action. You could possibly work with a CEO of a company. Your idea can be well constructed and built, with details and budget control, with supply lists and team required but your biggest aim, to reach the CEO, can destroy your hope if you haven't prepared for it. A path to reach every single recipient should also be mapped out.

You have the idea but you also need the backing of your boss, your peers and maybe someone in another organization for that idea to work. Thus, communication with everyone concerned is vital if you want to avoid any kind of misunderstanding. Remember that communication shares the idea and communicating with the right people may be vital to your task. If you are indecisive about whom to pitch your idea to, ask around. You could have a well-structured idea but until you know who to share it with, it is ineffective.

Some ideas can take weeks or months to be fully prepared. Never worry or tense over the time period unless you have a deadline. If you do have a deadline, always prepare your work so that you are ready in advance, so that if you need to make last minute changes, you can.

Listening to other ideas

If you have an idea, it's a good idea to share it with the right people and remember all the usual rules of communication. Listen to their ideas as they may enhance your original idea. How does your team feel about the idea? What do they think? How do they view the situation? All of these things matter.

What is their perspective? What roles are they interested in? As someone said "The most powerful person in the organization might share none of your philosophy, but the 3rd or 4th most powerful person might. The latter is going to be a better place to start."

This shows just how important communication is to the overall concept of pitching. Listening is a huge part of communication in general, which shows that effective communication is required not just in the act of pitching the idea to prospects, but in the creation of their idea as well.

Structure

This is where you increase your caffeine intake and want to avoid a mirror. Always use Ari Blenkhorn's 3 levels of depth breakdown: 5 seconds, 30 seconds, and 5 minutes. The 5-second level is to refine your idea in order to explain the entire concept in 5 seconds. This does not bore the person questioning you and maintains a professional status. Do not convince yourself that your idea is too complicated or advanced to be explained in 5 seconds.

The 30-second and 5 minute levels come out of the 5-second level naturally. In 30 seconds you can elaborate on what you said in 5 seconds. You do not have to worry about what to say in 5 minutes because chances are you will run out of audience during the first two levels. Some people, however, require written pitches. This gives you a chance to ignore the 3 level rules and simply write in complete depth.

As long as you have the right material and resources, you will achieve what you described in 5 seconds. Sometimes having a peer/partner can make things easier. Pitching will be easier as a team because, keeping aside the level rule, if you forget or panic, your partner will be there to further guide the questioning audience.

Testing

The longer you stick with your idea, the more your ego is likely to let you down. Find people to test your ideas on because they can help you to see any flaws or to improve your idea. Get them to ask you questions because there may be questions you didn't even think about that alter your perception of the idea.

If you have to pitch an idea and are worried about your approach or your communication skills, practice in front of a mirror and then try it on family members to see how they accept what it is that you are proposing. If they know that it's so that you improve your work position, they will be happy to help.

When it comes to actually pitching, do not hesitate. If you are well prepared the actual pitching takes very less effort. People who find the need to use tricks and manipulation are usually those whose egos are too big. Do not worry about the pitching as long as you are calm and direct. Also, be willing to listen to others. Listen to their questions and do not rush into answering questions without understanding the full implication of the question.

Learn to accept failure because not all business ideas will work. The communicator who can accept failure leaves themselves open to new ideas and that's always healthy. Listen to what others have to say and use that to help you to realize other ideas that are more valid and acceptable to everyone. The thing with this is that when you put trust in other people's ideas as being better than yours and give them credit for it, you increase your professionalism and your communication skills at the same time.

When all fails, the best option is to do it yourself. A lot of books are self published and businesses have started out small and been made larger. Low budget films have become successful and designers that believed in themselves have really made a name for themselves through that belief in their own ideas. It is very possible that your ideas are good and if you have the finance to back those ideas and believe in them enough, going independent may be your only alternative. Do not feel that your idea being rejected should stop you in your tracks.

Ross Elkins

Chapter 20: How to Get Over Stage Fright

The fear of performing on stage is relatively common. In fact, most people feel a degree of nervousness and apprehension when getting ready to perform in public. However, if you are nervous to the point where you start to dread facing your audience and are filled with discomfort and anxiousness at the thought of being in the public eye, or at being the center of attention, you might be experiencing a form of acute stage fright.

To deal with or to overcome your stage fright, you first need to assess what exactly it is that you're trying to fix. As with most phobias, there are degrees of stage fright and unless you figure out your trigger or the extent to which you are affected by your fear, you won't be able to fix the problem.

Performance anxiety and phobias of this nature are the top most common phobias in the United States. There are many forms of stage fright. Common and treatable forms include performance anxiety. Stage fright is a form of performance anxiety. Some people, whose career demands it, need to deal with stage fright on a common or even daily basis. You may be a seasoned actor or musician but being on the stage in front of others can fill you with anxiety. An athlete, no matter how senior or well trained, may falter while performing in the public eye because he/she may be experiencing some form of stage fright. From this, one might deduce that stage fright does not necessarily have to include any form of verbal communication at all. Athletes, dancers, etc. can also experience this uneasy phobia and there is no verbal communication involved in these professions.

Stage fright or performance anxiety is quite treatable if the people suffering with it have an open mind about it. People with stage fright try to avoid performing/appearing on stage if they can help it because their fear limits them and starts negative emotions in their mind. They view stage fright as an impairment and fear that they cannot overcome the problem.

Individuals may have different triggers. Stage fright can be neatly divided into four categories.

1. People who are acutely fearful of being on stage and go out of their way to avoid it. This sometimes means that their stage fright starts dictating the choices they make in life. They may avoid taking classes that interest them, as they fear they may be discussion based or feel that they may at some point have to take the stage during the course.

2. People who don't let their stage fright dictate their life choices, but are nevertheless anxious about appearing on stage and never feel secure and fully confident in the situation. For example, you are nominated to make a toast at a wedding. While you may feel anxious about making a mistake, saying the wrong thing or even appearing stupid in front of a crowd, you understand the delicateness of the situation and speak up in spite of your fear, however uneasy you may feel.

3. People whose professional success calls for them to speak or perform in public even if they'd rather not. For instance, an extremely successful businessman may have to address potential entrepreneurs and their form of stage fright may cause them to resent speaking.

4. People who work with creative expression such as artists, standup comedians, actors and athletes. While they may be good at what they do they are not immune to stage fright. They may yearn to flaunt their creativity in front of an audience but may be conscious about how the audience will receive them.

Solving the problem is a long and arduous process. The first step to solving a problem understands it, and that is what you do by breaking stage fright down into four categories. By doing this you are able to digest your stage fright as a smaller problem thus making it a lot easier to understand. You may even fear that your voice will not carry sufficiently for the space that you need to speak in.

Now that you have successfully understood what stage fright is, you can begin to heal yourself and get over it. Stage fright is a huge obstacle to successful communication. It does not just apply to the stage; it applies to all sorts of high-pressure situations such as board meetings, presentations, even asking a girl out on a date. Indeed, for a lot of people for whom communication is not their strong suit, crippling stage fright would mar any form of communication whatsoever.

Hence, in order to begin communicating in an effective manner it is important to get over stage fright. Here are ten tips you can use to help yourself do that:

1. Focus: or rather, shift the focus. Stage fright tends to be as debilitating as it is due to the fact that we fixate on it so much. When we are attempting to communicate, we should focus on the task that we are attempting to do rather than focus on how nervous we are doing it. Focus on the words you say and how you say them. Your stage fright is there no matter

what, paying it so much attention is not going to do anybody any good, least of all you.

2. Don't think about what might go wrong. Instead, focus on what you have to get right. Anything can go wrong at any time. Even problems as massive as an earthquake can occur while you are attempting to ask that beautiful girl out, and there is absolutely nothing you can do about it. You might think that this is worrying, but in fact the opposite is true. Since you can't do anything about it, why worry about it? Instead, you should try to focus on things that will calm you. A lot of people use meditation before speaking to help to create calm.

3. Avoid self-doubt: as you approach the situation where you are going to have to communicate, chances are that you are going to be racked with self-doubt. You are going to think about all of the negative things about yourself. These things might be your weight, your face, your hair, your voice or any aspect of yourself that you are, for some reason, conscious about. All you have to do is refuse. Refuse the self-doubt entry into your headspace. Focus instead on the task at hand and within no time you are going to effortlessly begin to communicate.

4. Meditate. As stated above, one of the most effective ways to calm yourself before you have to undertake a momentous communication moment is to meditate. Meditation calms you and clears your mind. It allows you to think about what you need to be thinking about. Alternatively, you can do anything that involves deep breathing and you will be surprised at just how calm it makes you. Exercise has the added advantage of filling up your brain with serotonin, a feel good chemical that will help you feel elated and excited, which will help you overcome your stage fright and self-doubt.

5. Stay healthy. A lot of stage fright isn't just psychological. Your lifestyle has a huge impact on how nervous you get when you are on stage, whether the stage is metaphorical or literal. One of the biggest contributors to stage fright is what you eat, or more accurately what you drink. Caffeine makes you jittery, so avoid it as much as possible before getting on stage. Alcohol may make you feel calm superficially, but it is only going to deaden your senses, which will make it even more difficult to focus on the task at hand. Additionally, sugar has the same effect on stage fright as caffeine so avoid it at all costs.

6. Picture success. You are a strong person; believe that. Nothing is more crippling to successful communication than self doubt. No one is perfect at communication, so you don't have to feel ashamed about the fact that you are, in some way, not as effective at communicating as everybody around you. Picture your success, imagine what it will feel like when that girl says yes, or when your boss smiles in approval. Whatever happens after you finish communicating, picturing success will at least help you get through the process of communicating itself.

7. Practice: that's right. Even if your stage fright has nothing to do with an actual play being performed on an actual stage, there is nothing better than practice to help you get through something that you are nervous about. No matter what it is that you are going to be saying or whom you are going to be saying it to, try to write a script of what you are going to say and practice it. Try to practice out loud in front of a mirror. This will allow you to see yourself and notice any aspects of your posture or body language that you find less than top notch. You can alter these aspects of yourself then and there, allowing you to be confident when you finally

get to the big moment and start communicating with the important people in your life.

8. Connect. Whoever it is that you are talking to, it is important that you connect with them in whatever way you can. Before you speak, look them in the eye and smile. This makes you seem more human and is something that will help you overcome the barriers to communicating effectively that exist for you. The basic logic behind this is seeing the person you are communicating with as a human, not as an obstacle that you need to overcome.

9. Mind your posture. Often people don't react well to what you are saying. This often compounds your stage fright and increases it exponentially. However, the other person's reaction to you is often not because of what you said or how you said it but because of your posture. Do not invade people's personal space. Try to stand an arm's length away while talking. Additionally, look them in the eye, adopt a posture that is warm and welcoming and speak in even tones.

10. Accept yourself. You are the best you that you can be. Nobody is perfect, not you and

not the person that you are going to talk to. You will never be perfect, and that's okay because perfect is boring. Accept your flaws and remember that trying to be like someone else will make you come across as disingenuous. The best course of action is to just be yourself.

Chapter 21: Common Barriers to Effective Communication and How to Overcome Them

Components in Communication

Have you ever asked why a few individuals can convey so well while others neglect to convey the desired information? What are the components that must be present in the process of communication before it can be fruitful and compelling? All things considered, communication has been characterized as the demonstration of giving, getting or trading data, thoughts and conclusions so that the message is totally comprehended by both sides. Moreover, in a process of communication, there must be a sender who talks or communicates something specific, and a collector who listens or gets the message. The sender communicates something specific on account of a certain goal. The collector of the message tries to comprehend and decipher the message sent. He then gives input to the first sender, who thusly deciphers the information. This procedure, rehashed constantly, constitutes the process of communication.

Plainly, there are a few noteworthy components in the communication process. These are: the sender, message, channel, beneficiary, input, and setting. There is both a speaker with the expectation to pass on a message and a listener who has the responsibility of gathering information that has been said.

Along these lines, listening abilities are pretty much as critical as talking aptitudes all together for communication to be considered successful.

This implies that on the off chance that you need to communicate as the need should arise precisely, you have to consider these three things:

• The message;

• The group of onlookers or collector; and

• How the message is prone to be gotten.

A message is just considered effectively conveyed when both the sender and, the collector see and comprehend it in the same way. On the off chance that this does not happen, then there may be a breakdown in communication, which might at last hinder you understanding your objectives.

Components Affecting Communication

As specified prior, successful communication is like a two-way handle, however there are various variables that may disturb this procedure and influence the general translation and comprehension of what was imparted. Heap issues can appear at the changed phases of the process of communication. These can identify with any of the components included: the sender, message, channel, recipient, criticism, and the setting. It is thusly essential to see a portion of the variables that influence communication so you can attempt to convey the desired information with insignificant misconception and disarray. The following are some conceivable issue zones that may swing out to be obstructions to successful communication and suggestions of practices in order to deal with them:

(a) Status/Role

The sender and beneficiary of a message may be of equivalent status inside of a chain of importance (e.g. administrators in an association) or they may be at distinctive levels (e.g. supervisor/representative, speaker/understudy, entrepreneur/customers). This distinction in status some of the time influences the viability of the correspondence process.

To avoid ineffective communication in this kind of situation, people should acknowledge the status or role of the sender or the receiver by acknowledging his position and giving due respect. For example, if the communication is between employee and his boss, the employee should watch his words by being totally respectful to his boss and being careful in choosing his words by acting not too close. If however, the employee is the receiver, he should show undivided attention as to show acknowledgment, obedience and respect. As to the boss, respect to his subordinates is also a requirement. He must be clear and precise to what he is saying so the employees could understand him well. If the boss is put however in to the listening position, he should show consideration to the words of his subordinates and reply with important details so to check the effectiveness of the communication done.

(b) Cultural Differences

Social contrasts, both inside or outside the association (for instance, between departmental dealings and correspondence with outside associations on the other hand ethnic minorities) may obstruct the correspondence process.

When dealing with communication among different races or even culture it is important to have enough facts or knowledge about the other person you are communicating with. This kind of communication barrier is quite sensitive because you have to have a thorough idea of what you are saying before you turn out to speak. For example, you may be speaking with a newly met person, who is not of your same culture, let us say he came from a far country. You may try to limit your words if you do not exactly know what kind of culture he has back in their place. There are some culture wherein some jokes may be intensively offensive while on the others are not. You may try to consider being extra careful in communicating and sharing thoughts or ideas to people you are not familiar with culture.

(c) Choice of Communication Channels

Before you pick your correspondence channel, you ought to ask yourself whether the channel is proper for a specific reason and the individual/recipient you have as a main priority. Sending messages by means of wrong channels can convey wrong flags and wind up making perplexity.

This kind of communication barrier is highly important to consider. For example in a relationship between couples, some kind of communication can be easily and comfortably done through phone calls or texts. It is on the situation that they are just casually talking about their day to day activities. However, if a certain trouble occurs, it is not appropriate for the two to talk over the phone as the means of communication could not show their exact emotions that is much of importance for the situation to be okay.

In a formal business setup, some type of communication is done through emails or video chats. While it is efficient and less time consuming, some important business matters should still be done in personal meetings as the medium could not clearly depict all the emotions or other factors that the sender would want to deliver and the receiver as well could not be able to get in all the facts he would need. For example, a boss who would like to imply to his subordinate that what he is instructing should be done immediately due to grave reasons may be more effective to be done personally so that personal expressions could also be shown and the subordinate may be pushed more rather than reading an email without emotions included.

(d) Length of Communication

The length of the message likewise influences the correspondence process. You should make sure that it fills the need and is fitting for the beneficiary. Is the message too long or excessively short?

This type of factor or barrier entails clarity and preciseness of effective an efficient communication. Let us say for example if a manager calls for a quick meeting among his team, he should be well prepared, focused and well planned on time. If however he planned for a 30 minute meeting yet he did not prepare well, it might so happen that the meeting would take longer than he planned. Let us say he did not present the facts clearly, so questions for his subordinates may arise leading to take the meeting longer.

In some relationship communication, for example, a father scolding his three year old child, time should not be too long in order for his young child to understand his predicaments. However, a father speaking mature matters to his eighteen year old daughter could take a lot more time because of the capacity of his daughter, the receiver, to understand more.

(e) Use of Language

Poor decision of words or frail sentence structure additionally hampers correspondence. The same goes for improper accentuation. In relation with the prior barrier, cultural difference, being careful with the use of language is also a sensitive one. One factor is the use of grammar. In any language across the world, right use of grammar is important for effective communication. If you cannot form your sentence well then the right understanding may be compromised as to your receiver or the worst case is to deliver a different intention.

(f) Incapacities

Incapacities, for example, hindered sight, dyslexia and poor emotional well-being can likewise be obstructions to great correspondence, and ought to be taken into thought when assessing the viability of the correspondence process. You may need to utilize amplifiers, gesture based communication, amplifying frameworks, and images to allay issues brought on by incapacities.

People with certain incapacities tend to have more challenge in terms of communication. However, technology nowadays made it easier for them to communicate with others with a little bit of effort and training. Like for example, a deaf person has its own way of communicating due to his situation. Nonetheless, effective communication can still be achieved through proper training, experience, knowledge and effort.

(g) Known or Unknown Receiver

Whether the collector is known or obscure to you additionally assumes a noteworthy part in deciding the viability of your correspondence. A known beneficiary may be better ready to comprehend your message regardless of having inadequate data as both of you most likely have regular encounters and a shared schemata. An obscure recipient, then again, may require more data and time to decipher the message.

Just like the prior example with the person with different culture, an unknown person is definitely more challenging to communicate with rather than those persons you are already familiar with.

Take your family for example; it is normal that you do have a different style of communicating with them rather than speaking with your colleagues and friends. They say in every different group you have, you may have different communication style appropriate for them. There may be a certain group in which you should show more respect like your bosses and older family members rather than those friends or family members who are in your same age.

Whatever group or person you may be communicating with always take consideration your familiarity with them. Too much closeness may indicate better and easier communication and so may somehow be comfortable about it. However in dealing with unfamiliar people, always consider to be extra careful in choosing the right set of words.

(h) Individual Perceptions/Attitudes/Personalities

Some of the time, the strategy for correspondence needs to look into the receivers identity characteristics, age and favored style. The elderly and kids, case in point, have distinctive correspondence needs and inclinations when contrasted with youthful grown-ups. Is the recipient of your message a visual, sound-related, on the other hand kinesthetic kind of individual?

How would you think they will respond to your message? Can you adjust your correspondence style to suit theirs?

1. Atmosphere/Noise/Distraction

2. Our environment can now and again act like boundaries to compelling correspondence. A boisterous spot (a gathering, for example) generally puts a strain on oral correspondence as both the sender and the beneficiary need to put additional push to get the message crosswise over and guarantee that it is seen obviously and accurately.

(j) Clarity of Message

Is the message passed on in a reasonable or uncertain way? Are you précised? Always keep in mind that the true success of communication is based on the exact and right understanding of both parties. Not whether the communication channel is right or the way the information is delivered. Any communication is always a case to case basis.

The clarity of message is based on how precise you are in delivering the message, knowing your intentions and focus as you go along the communication process.

(k) Lack of Feedback

Input is critical as it empowers affirmation of comprehension to be made by both sides. The absence of input can some of the time make issues as it can prompt instability and disarray. At the point when picking the most suitable channel of correspondence, you ought to regard the accompanying:

(a) Consider all parts of the correspondence process (understanding, understanding, and criticism).

(b) Think precisely about conceivable boundaries.

(c) Evaluate the many-sided quality of the message and choose how it may be best passed on.

(d) Ask yourself these inquiries:

• Who? Characteristics of the receiver(s)

• Why? Purpose of the correspondence

• What? Content of the message

• How? Oral, composed, visual or a blend of every one of the three

• Where? Location of the meeting

• When? Timing/time farthest point/expected reaction time.

(e) Determine whether you are meeting or keeping in touch with the individuals concerned. Is the correspondence by means of vis-à-vis connection, phone, letter, email, reminder or a report?

(f) Decisions about the most fitting channel of correspondence moreover rely on upon elements, for example, expense, time, tradition, desperation what's more, whether they would be fitting or not.

Conclusion

Communication is a vital aspect of the world we live in and there's a very strong argument that it's the greatest desire that any human being has for themselves and for those around them. Communication opens doorways and it helps us to understand the world that we live in. We don't want to spend our lives looking at others and feeling like outsiders, so communicating with them is going to be our only option. If communicating plays such a crucial role in the world that we live in, shouldn't we be the best at it that we can be? I think that's absolutely the case.

You should approach the world that you live in with a sense of wonder and excitement so that you can't help but engage in it. In this book, I hope that I have given you the courage and the desire to really get out there and start getting to know everyone that you can. Whether you're looking for friendship, love, power, or wealth, communication is going to be an obstacle for you on the road to achieving what it is you want. Don't be afraid to really get aggressive with life and go for everything you desire. You should never let fear get in the way of what it is you want from life.

So, in conclusion, I want you to really take away from this book what it means to be really focus on communication. Whether you're talking or listening, I want you to really focus on the world around you and to take away from it everything that you want. Have the dedication and the willingness to invest yourself in someone that you don't know and take away everything that you can from that relationship with them. Don't be afraid to get out there and let the world see who you are. Be brave, put away your electronic gadgetry and start talking.

Complete Your Business Relationship Skills Education With a Click Away:

Management: Golden Nugget Methods to Manage Effectively - Teams, Personnel Management, Management Skills, and Conflict Resolution

Leadership: Elevate Yourself and Those Around You - Influence, Business Skills, Coaching, & Communication

Take Your Business Skills Further for Financial Freedom or Corporate Dominance:

Small Business: EXACT BLUEPRINT on How to Start a Business - Home Business, Entrepreneur, and Small Business Marketing

Marketing: Golden Nuggets to Market Effectively - Internet Marketing, E-Commerce, Advertising & Web Marketing

Sales: Foolproof Method to CRUSH Your Numbers - Selling, Sales Techniques, and Sales Strategy

Made in the USA
San Bernardino, CA
30 April 2016